bundles
of fun

Karen Snyder

©2006 Karen Snyder

Published by

kp books
An Imprint of F+W Publications

700 East State Street • Iola, WI 54990-0001
715-445-2214 • 888-457-2873

Our toll-free number to place an order or obtain
a free catalog is (800) 258-0929.

Library of Congress Catalog Number: 2005935070

ISBN: 0-89689-230-1

Edited by Sarah Brown
Designed by Emily Adler

Printed in China

dedication

This book is dedicated to Connie Nason, Monica Solorio-Snow, Cortné Stricker and Melinda Crowley, who came to my rescue in my hour of need.

Sherry,
I hope this
book brings you
Bundles of Fun!
Karen Snyder

acknowledgments

I would like to thank the following wonderful people who helped make this book possible:

- Darlene Zimmerman for recommending KP Books and answering my many questions.
- Julie Stephani for walking me through the steps to becoming an author.
- Sarah Brown for her editing skills and patience.
- Emily Adler for the beautiful design of this book.
- My sister, Sally Paxton, and my mother, Bette Snyder, for their advice on grammar and punctuation.
- Beverly Wakeman for sharing her skill with the Big Stitch Technique.
- Laura Fadden, Susan Olson, Robin Anderson and Kathy Sasso for late night brainstorming.
- The women who so willingly made quilts for the book: Patty Stoltz, Gail Messick, Pat Hall, Darlene Zimmerman, Monica Solorio-Snow, Peggy Christenson, Ethel Knapp, Melinda Crowley, Cortné Stricker, Janet King, Joan Stoltz, Beverly Wakeman, Connie Nason and Karen Harmon. Who knew I had so many good friends!
- My husband, Bob Hamilton, and the rest of my family for believing in me.

table of contents

[6] Introduction

[8] General Instructions

[8] Prewashing Fabrics

[9] Cutting

[10] Seam Allowance

[10] Pressing

[11] Borders

[11] Battings

[12] Layering and Basting

[12] Quilting

[12] Binding

[13] Labeling

[14] Twelve Easy Pieces

[24] Dozen Roses

[32] Twelve O'clock Rock

[44] Baker's Dozen

[52] Twelfth Night

[60] Two Twelve Packs

[72] Midnight Cowboy

[80] Twelve Step Program

[90] Twelve Drummers Drumming

[100] Cheaper by the Dozen

[110] Until the Twelfth of Never

[118] Vitamin B-12

[128] Resources

[128] About the Author

introduction

This book is for those of you who love to pick up fat quarter bundles when you visit a quilt shop. Whether it's a keepsake to remember a visit to a shop far away from home, or a bundle from a local haunt that caught your eye, they can be irresistible. It may be a bundle of the most delicious, soft florals, cheery polka dots or adventurous frogs. The fabrics may be rolled into a bundle, fanned out on a piece of cardboard or stacked into a star. Often they are folded and packaged in such a way that you never want to untie the ribbon holding them together. I have a few of those special bundles decorating my own quilt room.

Buying fat quarter bundles takes the stress out of choosing fabrics that go together. Pre-bundled fat quarters usually contain fabrics that are coordinated by color or theme. You can find bundles of Civil War fabrics, cowboy fabrics, batiks, Depression-era reproductions, novelty prints and so much more. It's not unusual to find bundles from a single fabric collection or one designer. When you pick up a bundle of fat quarters and love the way the fabrics look, you're assured that they will work together in a quilt. Of course, if you're one of those quilters who loves to audition numerous fabrics, you can pick out your own individual fat quarters for your projects. Most quilt shops have shelves or baskets full of them. Many will even cut fat quarters from the bolt. Or how about your stash? I don't know a quilter anywhere who hasn't purchased at least a few fat quarters that have been taken home and set aside for some future project. Maybe you'll want to choose from those.

Because at the very least you are using twelve fabrics to make the projects in this book, the look of the quilts will be very scrappy. The fabrics you choose can really influence the feel or theme of your quilt. My favorite fabrics to work with are 1930s reproductions, but I also love florals, cowboy prints, polka dots and novelties. You can personalize any of the patterns in this book to fit your favorite theme.

Some of the quilts in the book only require the twelve fat quarters and some border fabric. Others require the addition of a background or accent fabric. I hope they all inspire you to grab a fat quarter pack and have bundles of fun!

what are fat quarters?

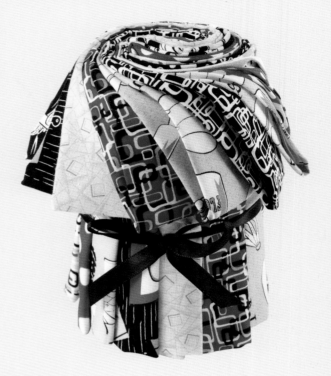

A fat quarter and a regular quarter yard of fabric have the same surface area, but fat quarters are often more suitable for cutting the patches necessary for quilting.

A quarter yard of fabric is a 9" cut from selvedge to selvedge, yielding a piece approximately 9" x 44". A fat quarter is made by first cutting ½ yard of fabric, or 18" from selvedge to selvedge. This piece is then cut in half along the fold line, yielding a piece that is approximately 18" x 22". Both pieces are equal in area, but fat quarters are often more suitable for cutting the shapes necessary for a quilt project.

why fat quarters?

Aside from the appeal of those neatly wrapped and tied bundles on display in the quilt shop, fat quarters have several advantages. The pieces are easier to handle than a long, skinny ¼-yard cut. Fat quarters are easier to stack on your cutting mat and easier to rotary cut. When making a long cut, it's easy to let your ruler pivot under your hand, causing cutting errors. With fat quarters, you're making shorter cuts and it's easier to keep your ruler stable.

When squaring up fat quarters, there is less waste. If you are squaring up a piece of fabric that is cut from selvedge to selvedge, you could lose 1"-2" or more of fabric. That loss is reduced when using fat quarters.

fabric selection

Using fat quarter bundles can eliminate a lot of the stress when it's time to pick fabrics for your next project. You don't have to match the fabrics in your project to those shown in the illustrations in this book. That's part of the joy of quilting — making a quilt that is uniquely your own. Just because I chose to make Twelve Easy Pieces from floral fabrics, you shouldn't hesitate to make it from hot rod prints or Civil War reproductions. In fact, if I were making quilts just to please myself, every quilt in this book would be made with 1930s reproduction fabrics — and they would all look great! So, set yourself free. Start by picking a bundle of fat quarters that you like, then pick a project that appeals to you — even if the sample in the book is made from something totally different. The results will be wonderful and you will have created a quilt that is truly your own!

Occasionally when you buy a fat quarter bundle or a kit, there may be one fabric in the package that you just don't like. Feel free to take it out! Don't be restricted by the bundle you choose. These are scrappy quilts, and it's okay to substitute another fat quarter from your stash or from the quilt shop.

And what if you should make a mistake when cutting? Just grab another fat quarter and add it to the mix. That's the beauty of scrap quilts. I doubt if any of your friends or the recipients of your quilts are going to count how many different fabrics you used.

quilt sizes

Because all of the quilts in the book start with a bundle of twelve fat quarters, most of the quilts are lap size. These are perfect for couch quilts, TV quilts and bed toppers. Some of the quilts — the ones that use more background or accent fabric — are larger.

It's easy to adjust the size of any of the quilts in the book if you want them larger. You could easily start with 18 fat quarters, or even 24. Just be sure to increase the yardage for your background or accent fabric, and the fabric for your borders.

You could also make the quilts smaller by using fewer fat quarters, or follow the suggestions in Two Twelve Packs, and make two quilts instead of one. This is a perfect technique if you have a lot of quilts to make as gifts for little ones.

I've taught many beginners to quilt, and I always tell them that there are only four steps to becoming a successful quilter:

[1] Accurate cutting.

[2] ¼" seam allowance.

[3] Good pressing techniques.

[4] Measuring through the middle when adding your borders.

Of course, you still need to quilt and bind your project, but if you pay attention to these four principles, your seams will match and your quilt top will lay flat.

prewashing fabrics

To wash or not to wash — that is the question. If you buy good quality cotton fabric, prewashing is not a necessity. I prefer not to wash my fabrics for a couple of reasons. First, I like the crispness of unwashed fabric. If you wash your fabrics, you remove the sizing. Secondly, I don't always have time. Often when I get a new bundle of fabrics, I just can't wait to cut into them! If I take the time to prewash, the inspiration may be gone! Lastly, I like the look that I get when I wash a quilt and it puckers up just a bit around my quilting stitches.

For those of you who do prewash, here are some tips. Because you'll be working with fat quarters, which are relatively small pieces of fabric, you don't want to just toss them into the washer and dryer. You risk losing too much fabric due to frayed edges. Shrinkage is minimal with good quality cotton fabrics. The main reason for prewashing is to remove any excess dye. You can do this easily without sending your fabrics for a spin in the washer and a tumble in the dryer. Follow these guidelines for prewashing your fat quarters:

[1] Fill your sink or a basin with tepid water. Put your fat quarters into the water one or two at a time, and swish them around. If you notice a lot of dye being released, change the water and repeat until the water stays clear.

[2] Place your fat quarters, a few at a time, on a towel. Roll the towel around them, squeeze to remove excess moisture, then drape them on anything handy until they are nearly dry.

[3] When the fabrics are still damp, iron them with a dry iron until they are completely dry. If you wait too long, and the fabric is completely dry, just spray them with a mist of water, wait a few minutes, then iron.

[4] You may want to use some spray sizing on your fabrics once you have pressed them dry. The sizing will give your fabrics body and make them easier to cut and to stitch.

cutting

Accurate cutting is the first step in making quilts that go together easily and lay flat. Proper tools make cutting easy. Be sure that your rotary cutter has a sharp blade with no nicks, that you have a ruler that is at least 24" long and that your mat is free of grooves.

The most common problem when cutting is letting the ruler wiggle as you make your cut. To avoid this, spread your fingers apart and place the fingertips on the half of the ruler that is closest to you. Do not lay your palm flat on the ruler. Lay your rotary cutter next to the ruler and cut about halfway across your fabric. Leaving your cutter in place, walk the fingers of the hand that is on the ruler up to the half of the ruler that is farthest from you. Press downward with your fingertips and continue making the cut.

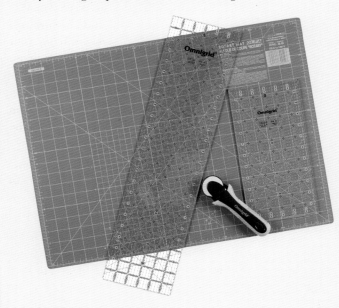

Proper tools make cutting easy.

Get familiar with your cutting tools and learn to read your ruler correctly. If you are cutting a lot of strips that are the same size, it can be helpful to put a narrow piece of masking tape on the back of the ruler at the proper measurement. That way you can quickly see that you are lining up properly.

Did you know that your index finger should be placed on the top of your rotary cutter? Every brand of rotary cutter has a place for your index finger. If you grip your cutter like a two-year-old learning to eat with a spoon, and make your cuts with all your fingers wrapped around the handle, your wrist is twisted and your hand is in an awkward position. By placing your index finger on the top of your cutter, you have a straight line from your elbow. This is ergonomically correct and won't lead to problems with your wrist or elbow.

When working with fat quarters, you are working with fairly small pieces of fabric. Fat quarters are approximately 18" x 22". The 22" measurement, however, usually includes the selvedge. This is the edge where the fabric yarns are woven back, and it needs to be trimmed off. All of the instructions in the book tell you which side of your fat quarter should be across the bottom edge of your cutting mat when you begin cutting. While you will want to even the edges of your fat quarters and trim away the selvedge, be conservative when trimming.

You can speed your cutting by layering your fat quarters and cutting several at a time. For the sake of accuracy, I don't like to layer more than four fat quarters. When layering several fat quarters, align the edges with the selvedge. Depending on the pattern instructions, place this edge either at the top or the right side of your cutting mat. Trim the left edge of the fat quarters so they are even before beginning to cut.

seam allowance

Once you've cut your pieces accurately, it is important to sew them together using ¼" seams. Many sewing machines come with a ¼" foot, or a special ¼" foot can be purchased for them. If you quilt a lot, you may want to consider this. If you do not have a ¼" foot, lay your acrylic ruler under your needle. Slowly, by hand, lower your needle until it just rests on the ¼" mark. Place a piece of masking tape on your machine to mark along the edge of ruler. Use this tape as a guide when sewing your seams.

To make sure that you are using your ¼" foot correctly, or that you have your masking tape in the correct position, do this experiment:

[1] Cut two 2" strips of fabric, about 3" long.

[2] Lay the strips together and sew along the long side with ¼" seam. Press.

[3] Use your ruler to measure the width of the piece. It should be 3½". If not, make adjustments and repeat the experiment.

pressing

Pressing is just what is says — pressing. You want to press your fabrics and your seams without distorting them. It requires a gentle touch to do this. Whether or not to use steam is a matter of personal preference, but be aware that you are more likely to distort your fabrics if you are using steam.

When quilting, seams are generally pressed to one side as opposed to being pressed open. When pressing seams to one side, it is very important to press from the front. Lay the pieced patches on the ironing board. Since you will usually want to press your seam toward the darker fabric, lay the pieced patch with the darker fabric on the top. This will automatically make the seam allowance lay toward the darker fabric. Give the seam a quick press to help marry the sewing threads to the fabric. Then gently lift the top layer of fabric. Use the side of the iron to lay it over and press. By pressing from the front in this manner, you will avoid leaving little folds or pleats at the seams. These little pleats can have an adverse effect when you join your blocks or rows together.

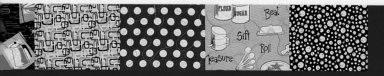

borders

Borders on a quilt act like a frame on a picture; they serve to contain the action going on in the body of the work. Often this can be accomplished with a narrow border of an accent fabric and a wider border that matches the tone and value of the blocks. You can also use borders to increase the size of the finished quilt. Each of the projects in the book gives suggestions for choosing appropriate borders.

While borders may be the finishing touch to your masterpiece, if applied incorrectly, they can cause problems. If you merely cut a long strip and start sewing it to the edges of your quilt top, the border strip has a tendency to "grow," and the quilt won't lay flat. This occurs because the edges of the quilt include numerous seams, which can become "unlocked" when you handle the quilt top. As you add the border to the edge of the top, each seam may open a little, causing the problem.

You can, however, create a quilt top that lays flat every time. It's as simple as measuring correctly and cutting the border strips the proper length before adding them.

[1] After piecing and assembling the quilt blocks, find a flat surface on which to lay the finished top. Using a tape measure, measure the length of the quilt *through the middle*. Cut two strips of border fabric this length.

[2] Find the center of the strip and the center of the quilt top. *Note:* To find the center, fold the fabric in half and finger press.

[3] Pin the border strip to the quilt top at the center point.

[4] Pin the top and bottom edge. Continue pinning every few inches, easing if necessary.

[5] Sew the seam with a ¼" seam allowance. Press toward the border fabric.

[6] Measure the width of the quilt top. Again, measure through the middle. This is what will assure that your finished top will lay flat. Cut two strips of border fabric this length.

[7] Find the centers, pin, stitch and press.

[8] If there are multiple borders, repeat the steps, cutting and sewing the lengthwise borders first.

battings

Batting is available in a variety of materials. It can be made from natural fibers like cotton, wool or even silk. It can also be made from polyester or a combination of a natural fiber and polyester, as well. When choosing batting, you must also consider the different weights, thicknesses and lofts. I use mostly cotton blends because I like the flat look and ease of care that they provide. Occasionally, I use a polyester bat, but look for one that drapes well and doesn't have too much loft.

layering and basting

Once your quilt top is complete, you will need to make a quilt "sandwich" before you begin quilting. The quilt sandwich is made up of the quilt back, batting and the pieced top. **The backing and batting should be at least 4" larger than the quilt top.**

[1] After doing any necessary piecing of the backing fabric, tape the fabric wrong-side up to a flat surface, pulling it taut.

[2] Lay the batting over the backing and smooth out any wrinkles.

[3] Lay the well-pressed quilt top right-side up on top of the batting.

[4] If hand quilting, baste with long running stitches. If machine quilting, baste with safety pins.

quilting

Quilting is the finishing touch in quiltmaking. All of the quilts in the book give suggestions for quilting designs but feel free to experiment on your own. If you aren't experienced in quilting by hand or machine, there are many good books available on the subject.

binding

[1] Cut binding strips 2¼" wide.

[2] After cutting the required number of strips, piece them together with diagonal seams.

[3] Press the seams open.

[4] Press the binding in half lengthwise, wrong sides together.

[5] Trim the excess batting and backing from the quilt top.

[6] Beginning in the middle of one edge of the quilt, place the folded binding strip, right sides together, along the edge of the quilt. The raw edges of the binding and the raw edges of the quilt should be together. Pin one side.

[7] Beginning 6" or 7" from the end of the binding strip, stitch with a ¼" seam. Stop stitching ¼" from the corner.

[8] Backstitch.

[9] Pivot the quilt. Fold the binding strip up at a 45-degree angle, then back down.

[10] Begin sewing at the top edge of the quilt.

[11] Continue around all four corners. Stop stitching approximately 3" from the beginning of the strip. This will leave about 9" of binding unsewn.

[12] In the middle of this space, fold back the loose ends of the strips so they meet.

[13] Mark a dot along the fold at this point.

[14] Open the binding strips.

[15] Pivot, aligning the dots, and sew the strips together with a diagonal seam.

[16] Trim the excess binding and attach the unsewn area to the quilt.

[17] Fold the binding over the raw edge of the quilt so that it covers the machine stitching on the back side.

[18] Stitch in place using a blind stitch. A miter will form at the corners of your quilt.

labeling

I can't stress enough how important it is to label your quilts. Have you ever had the frustration of looking through old family photograph albums and wondering about the ancestors who stare out at you from faded photographs? I feel the same way when I look at antique and vintage quilts.

Quilts have a story to tell. Even unlabeled quilts tell a story. The fabrics used in them are a clue to their age. The precision of the stitching is an indication of the maker's skill. The amount of wear tells whether the quilt was used for utility or display. Missing is the who, what and where; who made the quilt, what was the occasion and where did the quiltmaker live? A simple label stitched to the back of a quilt can answer all of these questions.

Quilt labels can be simple or elaborate. A piece of muslin with the pertinent information written in permanent ink and whipstitched to the back of the quilt will suffice. If you are feeling more creative, you can embroider a label by hand or machine and embellish it with additional needlework. Photos transferred to fabric add a personal touch to a quilt. Decorative fabric labels are also available. These often have a floral design around the border and a blank area for you to add your personal information.

My favorite way to make a label is:

[1] Type your information into a word processing program on your computer. Use a font and type size that is easy to read. A type size of 16 - 24 is a good choice.

[2] Print the information and tape the paper to a desk or table.

[3] Tape an unwashed piece of muslin over the paper.

[4] Using a fine-point permanent pen, trace over the letters.

[5] Remove the tape. Press edges under ¼".

[6] Stitch the label to the back of the quilt. Future generations will thank you!

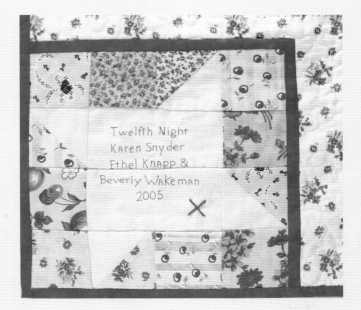

twelve easy pieces

This is the quilt that started it all. At our shop, we were looking for a quilt that would use 12 fat quarters and go together quickly. It really doesn't get much easier than this. This quilt is made using 6" squares surrounded by two borders and finished with a scrappy binding. When you make the quilt, you will have nine squares left over. They can easily be made into a fun doll quilt to match your big quilt, which you can give to a favorite little friend.

The geometric prints and strong colors of this quilt give it a fun, bold look.
PIECED BY PAT HALL AND QUILTED BY THE AUTHOR, 2003.

variations

A bundle of flannel fabrics with a floral motif make a warm, charming quilt.
PIECED AND QUILTED BY THE AUTHOR, 2005.

The wilderness fabrics used here give this quilt a more masculine feeling.
PIECED BY PATTY STOLTZ AND QUILTED BY THE AUTHOR, 2005.

choosing fabric

In this quilt, anything goes! You can pick up any bundle of 12 fat quarters and have success. If you choose a bundle of fat quarters that are the same in tone and scale, your finished quilt will have a blended feel. If the fabrics in your bundle have more contrast, the blocks in your quilt will stand out more. A bundle of soft floral fabrics will result in a pretty quilt. The blocks in this quilt are large, however, so don't overlook the possibility of using large-scale prints or bold colors.

For the inner border, a coordinating fabric a shade or two lighter or darker than those used in your blocks is a good choice. This gives your eye a place to rest. The outer border could be one of the fabrics used in the blocks of the quilt.

measurements

Quilt: 56" x 68"

Block: 6" square

fabric requirements

12 fat quarters

½ yd. inner border fabric

1¼ yd. outer border fabric

3½ yd. backing fabric

60" x 72" batting

NOTE: The binding is made from fat quarter strips.

cutting instructions

NOTE: Lay the 18" side of the fat quarter along the bottom edge of the cutting mat, selvedge to the top.

From each fat quarter, cut:

   2 (6½") strips; crosscut into 6 (6½") squares

   2 (2¼") strips for the binding

From the inner border fabric, cut:

   6 (2½") strips x width of fabric

From the outer border fabric, cut:

   7 (5½") strips x width of fabric

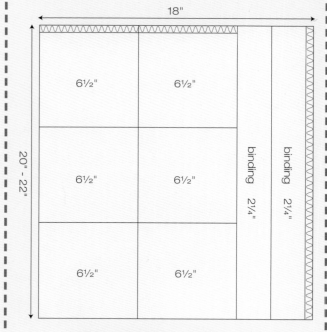

Fat quarter cutting diagram.

assemble the top

[1] Working on a design wall or on the floor, lay out the 6½" squares in nine rows of seven blocks each. Lay them out in a random fashion. *Note:* This is a scrappy quilt, so anything goes, but you will want to avoid having two like fabrics touching. You will have nine blocks left over. These can be used in your doll quilt.

[2] Once you have the blocks laid out in a pleasing manner, join the blocks together into rows.

[3] Press the seams in each row in opposite directions. This will allow the seams in each row to nest with the seams in the row below it.

[4] Join the rows together. Press.

add the borders

[1] Join the strips for the inner border together by sewing diagonal seams. Press open. Join all of the strips together until you have one long strip.

[2] Measure the quilt lengthwise *through the middle*. This will prevent you from having wavy borders. Mathematically this number would be 54½", but everyone's seam allowances vary, so be sure to measure.

[3] Cut two strips the length of the quilt.

[4] Attach one to each side of the quilt. Press.

[5] Measure the quilt crosswise *through the middle*. This measurement should be approximately 46½", but check your measurement to be sure.

[6] Cut two strips this length.

[7] Add the strips to the top and bottom of the quilt. Press.

[8] Repeat Steps 1-7 with the outer border fabric.

prepare the backing

[1] Cut the backing fabric into two equal pieces.

[2] Remove the selvedges and join the pieces together.

finish

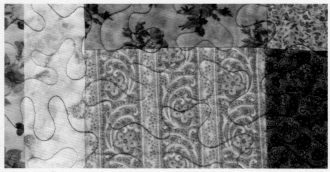

[1] Prepare your quilt sandwich following the Layering and Basting instructions on page 12.

[2] Quilt. The options for quilting this quilt are wide open. You may want to crosshatch through the squares or do a large meander. You can let the fabrics in the quilt influence your quilting design. When making this quilt from cowboy fabrics, we quilted it with loops and stars. With a floral design, a leaf pattern in the border helped set off the floral fabrics in the blocks. Let your imagination run wild!

bind

[1] Cut each of the binding strips in half to yield 48 strips 10" x 2½".

[2] Randomly join the strips together using diagonal seams. Press open. This will yield enough binding for both the lap quilt and the doll quilt.

[3] Bind following the Binding instructions on page 12.

label

Your quilt isn't finished until you've added a label. A simple label made from a scrap of muslin or white fabric is all it takes. Jot down your name, the date and where you live. If the quilt is a gift, put the recipient's name on the label. Whipstitch the label to the back of the quilt. Use some left-over binding to frame the label for a nice finishing touch.

Layout diagram.

bonus easy pieces doll quilt

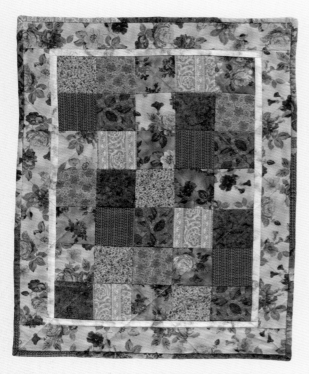

Leftover blocks make a charming doll quilt.
PIECED BY THE AUTHOR AND QUILTED BY CONNIE NASON, 2005.

You'll find it takes no time at all to turn the left-over blocks from Twelve Easy Pieces into the perfect doll quilt. In fact, you may find these are so fun to give away to children who visit, that you'll be collecting 6½" squares or searching your stash so you can make more. A small quilt like this is also a good size on which to practice your machine quilting.

measurements

Quilt: 18½" x 24"
Block: 2¾" square

fabric requirements

9 (6½") squares, either left over from the Twelve Easy Pieces quilt or gathered from another source

⅛ yd. inner border fabric

¼ yd. outer border fabric

⅔ yd. backing fabric

23" x 28" batting

cutting instructions

From each of the 6½" squares, cut:
    4 (3¼") squares; this will yield 36 squares
From the inner border fabric, cut:
    2 (1") strips x width of fabric
From the outer border fabric, cut:
    2 (2½") strips x width of fabric

assemble the top

[1] Follow the Twelve Easy Pieces assembly instructions on page 19, but lay out the squares in seven rows of five blocks each. This will use 35 squares, leaving you with one left over.

[2] Join the blocks together into rows.

[3] Press the seams in each row in opposite directions. This will allow the seams in each row to nest with the seams in the row below it.

[4] Join the rows together. Press.

add the borders

Refer to the Twelve Easy Pieces border instructions on page 19 to add the two borders, adding the narrow border (1") first, followed by the wider (2½") border.

prepare the backing

Cut the backing fabric into a 24" x 29" rectangle.

finish

[1] Prepare your quilt sandwich following the Layering and Basting instructions on page 12.

[2] Quilt. This is a great little piece on which to practice your machine quilting. A simple cross hatch makes a nice finish to this small quilt.

bind

There will be enough scrappy binding left from the lap quilt to bind the doll quilt. Bind following the Binding instructions on page 12.

label

Even a doll quilt deserves a label. The label, however, doesn't have to be on the back of the quilt. You could sign in one of the blocks on the front of the quilt if the fabric is light enough.

PIECED BY PATTY STOLTZ AND QUILTED BY JOAN STOLTZ, 2005.

dozen roses

A bundle of vivid floral prints was the inspiration for this quilt. It is one of the easiest quilts in the book, yet the results are quite stunning. It's a perfect pattern for showcasing those large-scale floral prints that are so appealing but so difficult to cut into. The strong diagonal layout gives order to the design, and the double borders help contain the action.

variations

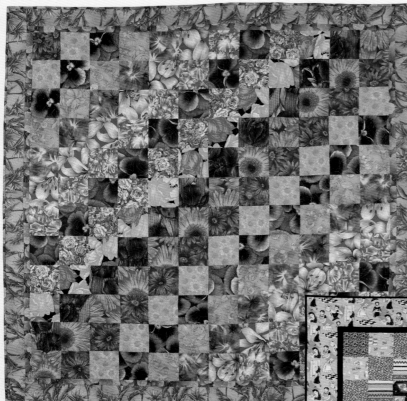

Bold floral fabrics awash with rich colors were the inspiration for this pattern.
PIECED BY GAIL MESSICK AND QUILTED BY THE AUTHOR, 2005.

Don't overlook novelty prints, like these retro kitchen prints, when making this quilt. Additional border fabric was needed to allow for the directional print and a slightly wider border in this sample.
PIECED AND QUILTED BY THE AUTHOR, 2005.

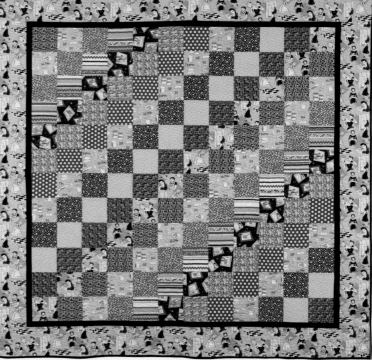

choosing fabric

Unlike many quilts, contrast doesn't need to be a consideration when making this pattern. Since the blocks, however, are not pieced, the fabrics will have to stand on their own. If you have a bundle of fat quarters that you're in love with, this may be just the quilt to use them in. You don't have to add any other fabric for background or accent.

There's no need to limit yourself to florals for this quilt. While fabrics with small prints work well here, the size and simplicity of the blocks lend themselves nicely to any large-scale design. It could be the perfect venue for nursery rhyme fabrics or other novelty prints.

measurements

Quilt: 62" square
Block: 4½" square

fabric requirements

12 fat quarters
⅓ yd. inner border fabric
⅞ yd. outer border fabric
3⅔ yd. backing fabric
½ yd. binding fabric
66" x 66" batting

cutting instructions

NOTE: Lay the 18" side of the fat quarter along the bottom edge of the cutting mat, selvedge to the top.

From each fat quarter, cut:
  3 (5") strips; crosscut into 12 (5") squares
From the inner border fabric, cut:
  6 (1½") strips x width of fabric
From the outer border fabric, cut:
  7 (3½") strips x width of fabric
From the binding fabric, cut:
  7 (2¼") strips x width of fabric

Fat quarter cutting diagram.

assemble the blocks

[1] Work on a design wall or on the floor. Refer to the layout diagram and the photographs; you will see that the blocks are placed in a diagonal pattern. Lay out the squares in twelve rows with twelve blocks in each row. You may want to experiment with your fabrics to see which squares look best next to each other.

[2] Once you have decided upon a layout, join the blocks together into rows.

[3] Press the seams in each row in opposite directions. This will allow the seams in each row to nest with the seams in the row below it.

[4] Join the rows together. Press.

add the borders

[1] Join the strips for the inner border together by sewing diagonal seams. Press open. Join all of the strips together until you have one long strip.

[2] Measure the quilt lengthwise *through the middle*. This will prevent you from having wavy borders. Mathematically this number would be 54½", but everyone's seam allowances vary, so be sure to measure.

[3] Cut two strips the length of the quilt.

[4] Attach one to each side of the quilt. Press.

[5] Measure the quilt crosswise *through the middle*. This measurement should be approximately 56½", but check your measurement to be sure.

[6] Cut two strips this length.

[7] Attach one to the top and one to the bottom of the quilt. Press.

[8] Repeat Steps 1-7 with the outer border fabric.

prepare the backing

[1] Cut the backing fabric into two equal pieces.

[2] Remove the selvedges and join the pieces together.

finish

[1] Prepare your quilt sandwich following the Layering and Basting instructions on page 12.

[2] Quilt. Depending on your fabric choice, the large squares could be the perfect area to do some creative quilting. On floral fabrics, you may choose to quilt a flower in the middle of each block and a continuous leaf in the border. If you used novelty prints, you may want to outline a certain motif. If your quilt just needs something simple, consider crosshatching diagonally through the blocks and into the borders.

bind

Bind following the Binding instructions on page 12.

label

Don't leave future generations wondering about the history of the quilts you make. Take a moment to document them. Choose a motif from your fabric to embellish the label. If you like to appliqué, you can embellish the label on a floral quilt; just cut a flower from a scrap of fabric and appliqué it to the label.

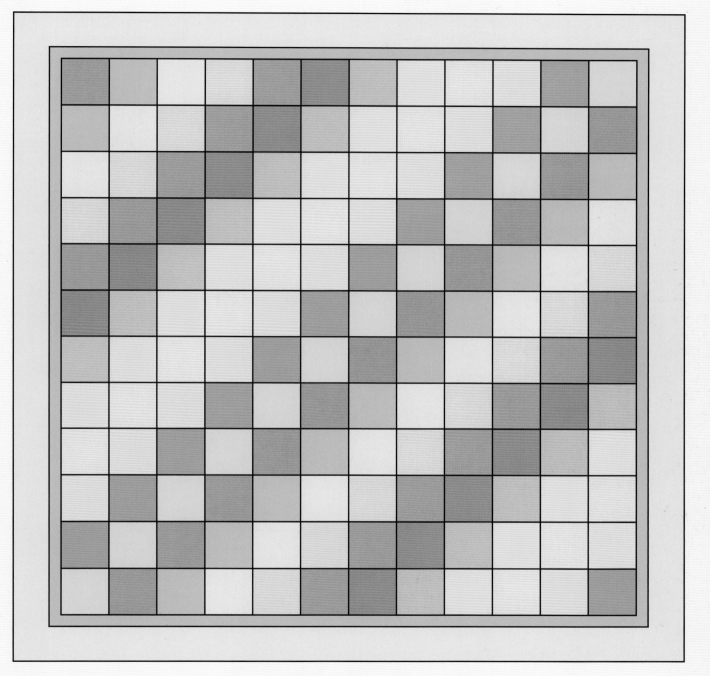

Layout diagram.

twelve o'clock rock

An antique quilt top in double pinks and cadet blues was the inspiration for this quilt. The design translated well when made with a bundle of 1930s reproduction fabrics. People often forget that fabrics from that era weren't just pastels. Quilts of the day often incorporated stronger colors such as red, screaming yellow, Nile green, deep lavender, blue and even orange! You'll have enough four-patch blocks left over from piecing this quilt to make an interesting pieced back or two pillowcases.

variations

The browns and pinks in this quilt recreate the look of the late 19th century.
PIECED BY DARLENE ZIMMERMAN AND QUILTED BY THE AUTHOR, 2005.

A variety of reds contrast nicely with the pastels in this quilt.
PIECED AND QUILTED BY THE AUTHOR, 2004.

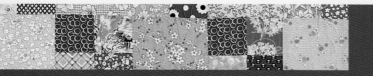

choosing fabric

The most important element in this quilt is the accent fabric. This is the fabric that creates the strong geometric pattern in the quilt. In order for them to stand out, the fabrics in your bundle should all have a similar value and the accent fabric should be considerably darker or lighter. You could also achieve the contrast by using a color that doesn't appear in your fat quarters. A bundle of floral fabrics with a green accent fabric would make a pretty quilt. Another possibility would be a bundle of black and white prints with a red accent. Let your bundle guide you!

A narrow inner border and a wider outer border finish this quilt nicely. For the inner border, choose something that will help separate the body of the quilt from the border. The outer border could be one of the fabrics in the quilt, or something that picks up the colors of the fat quarters.

measurements

Quilt: 59" x 75"

Block: 4" square

fabric requirements

12 fat quarters

1½ yd. accent fabric

⅜ yd. inner border fabric

1¼ yd. outer border fabric

4½ yd. backing fabric

½ yd. binding fabric

63" x 79" batting

cutting instructions

NOTE: Lay the 18" side of the fat quarter along the bottom edge of your cutting mat, selvedge to the top.

From each fat quarter, cut:

    2 (4½") strips; crosscut into 8 (4½") squares

    3 (2½") strips

From the accent fabric, cut:

    18 (2½") strips x width of fabric

From the inner border fabric, cut:

    6 (1½") strips x width of fabric

From the outer border fabric, cut:

    7 (5") strips x width of fabric

From the binding fabric, cut:

    7 (2¼") strips x width of fabric

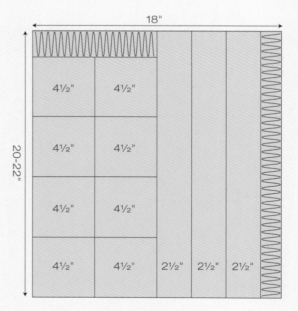

Fat quarter cutting diagram.

piece the blocks

Make the four-patch blocks:

[1] Cut each of the accent strips in half, so they are approximately 21"- 22" long. This way, they will be the right length to pair with the print strips cut from the fat quarters.

[2] Place a 2½" print strip and a 2½" accent strip right sides together.

[3] Sew along the long side using ¼" seam.

[4] Repeat until you have 36 strip sets.

[5] Press toward the accent fabric.

[6] Using a rotary cutter and ruler, cut the strip sets into 2½" segments. Each strip set should yield 8 segments.

[7] To make a four-patch block, randomly join two segments together, matching seams. Press. You will need a total of 96 four-patch blocks.

[5]
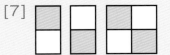

Make the strip sets.

[6]

Cut the segments.

[7]

Make the four-patch blocks.

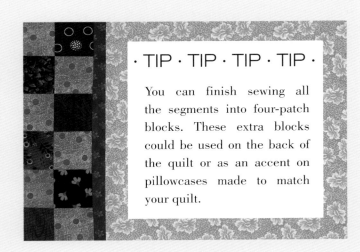

· TIP · TIP · TIP · TIP ·

You can finish sewing all the segments into four-patch blocks. These extra blocks could be used on the back of the quilt or as an accent on pillowcases made to match your quilt.

assemble the top

[1] Working on a design wall or on the floor, lay out the four-patch blocks and the 4½" squares. Be careful to turn the four-patch blocks so the accent fabric makes a diagonal design in the quilt. Refer to the layout diagram for the placement. Spread the 4½" squares throughout the quilt in a random fashion. You will want to avoid having two like fabrics touching.

[2] Once you have the blocks laid out in a pleasing manner, join the blocks together into rows.

[3] Press the seams in each row toward the plain squares. This will allow the seams in each row to nest with the seams in the row below it.

[4] Join the rows together. Press.

add the borders

[1] Join the strips for the inner border together by sewing diagonal seams. Press open. Join all of the strips together until you have one long strip.

[2] Measure the quilt lengthwise *through the middle*. This will prevent you from having wavy borders. Mathematically this number would be 64½", but everyone's seam allowances vary, so be sure to measure.

[3] Cut two strips the length of your quilt.

[4] Attach one to each side of the quilt. Press.

[5] Measure the quilt crosswise *through the middle*. This measurement should be approximately 50½", but check your measurement to be sure.

[6] Cut two strips this length.

[7] Attach one strip to the top and one strip to the bottom of the quilt. Press.

[8] Repeat Steps 1-7 with the outer border fabric.

prepare the backing

[1] Cut the backing fabric into two equal pieces.

[2] Remove selvedges.

[3] Split one piece in half lengthwise.

[4] Sew the split piece to either side of the other backing piece.

See Option 1 on page 42 to use the extra four-patch blocks on the back of your quilt.

See Option 1 on page 42 to use the extra four-patch blocks on the back of your quilt.

finish

[1] Prepare your quilt sandwich following the Layering and Basting instructions on page 12.

[2] Quilt. To make your accent fabric stand out even more, you could stipple this quilt in all the areas *except* the squares made from the accent fabric. Alternately, the strong diagonal lines of this quilt would contrast nicely with the curves of an allover feather motif.

bind

Bind following the Binding instructions on page 12.

----

label

Take time to make a label for your quilt. If you are married and have taken your husband's surname, you may want to include your maiden name in your signature. Future generations of genealogists will thank you!

Layout diagram.

using the extra four-patches

option 1: pieced back

There's no reason the back of your quilt shouldn't be as interesting as the front. The back of a quilt is the perfect place to use leftover blocks or scraps of fabric. On this quilt, you could use the four-patches to make long strips for an accent.

[1] Sew 20 four-patches together into one long strip.

[2] Repeat to make a second strip. Each strip will be approximately 80" long (the same length as the backing for your quilt).

[3] Before sewing the three pieces of backing fabric together, sew a strip of four-patches to each side of the widest backing segment.

[4] Sew the narrow backing segments to either side.

Use the four-patch segments on the back of the quilt.

option 2: accent pillowcases

It's always fun to make coordinating pillowcases for your quilts. Making them from matching fabrics is a nice touch, but when you have blocks left over, as you do in this quilt, your pillowcases will really make a statement!

Pillowcases that coordinate with your quilt offer a decorative touch. Extra four-patches form the cuff on this easy-to-assemble pillowcase.

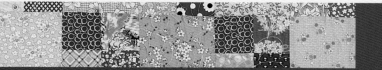

measurements

Pillowcase: 20" x 34"

fabric requirements

(For two pillowcases)

20 blocks left over from piecing Twelve O'clock Rock

2 yd. main fabric and cuff lining

⅛ yd. accent fabric

choosing fabric

If you've made your quilt from a bundle of fat quarters, you may not be able to match the fabric used in the body of the quilt. A perfect solution is to choose the same fabric for the main portion of your pillowcase as you used in the outer border of your quilt. The accent fabric in your pillowcase could be the same as the inner border of your quilt.

cutting instructions

From the main fabric, cut:
    2 (26½" x 40½") pieces for the pillowcase body
    2 (4½" x 40½") pieces for the cuff lining
From the accent fabric, cut:
    1 (1¼" x 40½") strip

assemble the pillowcases

[1] Sew 10 four-patch strips together into one long strip. This strip will measure 4½" x 40½".

[2] Sew a cuff lining to one side of the four-patch strip.

[3] Sew the accent strip to the other side of the four-patch strip.

[4] Sew the main body fabric to the accent strip. Press all seams toward the four-patch strip.

[5] Fold the pillowcase in half, right sides together. Stitch along two sides using ¼" seam.

[6] At the open end, press under ¼" on the cuff lining. Fold the cuff lining over the four-patch strip. Press. The cuff lining should cover the seam where the four-patch strip and the accent strip are joined. Pin in place.

[7] Hand stitch the cuff lining in place.

[8] Turn the pillowcase right-side out. Press.

[9] Repeat Steps 1-8 for a second pillowcase.

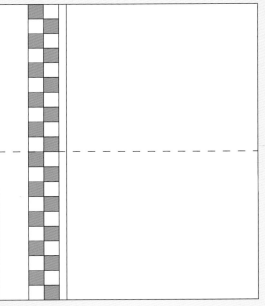

Make 2.

baker's dozen

This is a perfect pattern for using novelty fabrics. The entire quilt is made from two sizes of squares and sashing strips. What could be easier? A line of fruit and vegetable fabrics was the inspiration for this quilt. There were thirteen fabrics in the line, and I couldn't decide which one to leave out. I just had to have them all!

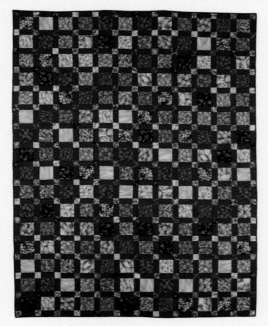

In this version of Baker's Dozen, the fruit and vegetable patches are sashed with a basket weave fabric, giving the quilt the look of bushels of produce at a farm stand.
PIECED AND QUILTED BY THE AUTHOR, 2005.

variations

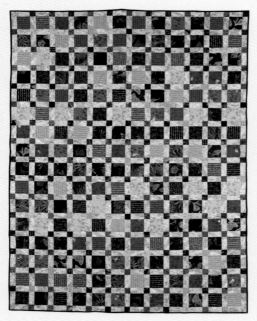

Because of its lighter tone, the sashing in the quilt recedes and allows the patches of Asian-inspired fabrics to dominate.
PIECED BY MONICA SOLORIO-SNOW AND QUILTED BY THE AUTHOR, 2005.

A serene appearance is achieved in this quilt by limiting the palette to two colors: red and black.
PIECED BY PEGGY CHRISTENSON AND QUILTED BY THE AUTHOR, 2005.

choosing fabric

Novelty prints work great in this pattern, as long as the scale isn't too large. A variety of produce prints is contained within the sashings created from a basket weave fabric. Novelty frog prints with a green lily-pad sashing, or hot rod prints with a flame fabric as the sashing, would be equally as fun. Choose a bundle of fat quarters, then look for a sashing fabric that will frame them nicely. Using the same fabric for your sashing and binding is a good option for this quilt.

measurements

Quilt: 61½" x 81½"
Block: 3½" square

fabric requirements

13 fat quarters
2½ yd. sashing fabric
3¾ yd. backing fabric
⅝ yd. binding fabric
66" x 85" batting

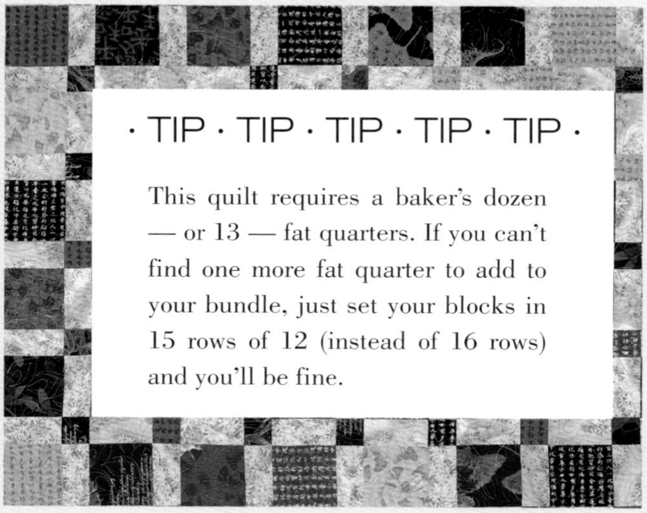

· TIP · TIP · TIP · TIP · TIP ·

This quilt requires a baker's dozen — or 13 — fat quarters. If you can't find one more fat quarter to add to your bundle, just set your blocks in 15 rows of 12 (instead of 16 rows) and you'll be fine.

cutting instructions

NOTE: Place the 20"-22" side of the fat quarter along the bottom edge of your cutting mat, selvedge at the right.

From each of the 13 fat quarters, cut:

4 (4") strips; crosscut into 15 (4") squares and 4 (2") squares

2 (2") strips; crosscut into 18 (2") squares

From the sashing fabric, cut:

42 (2") strips x width of fabric; crosscut into 2" x 4" rectangles

From the binding fabric, cut:

8 (2¼") strips x width of fabric

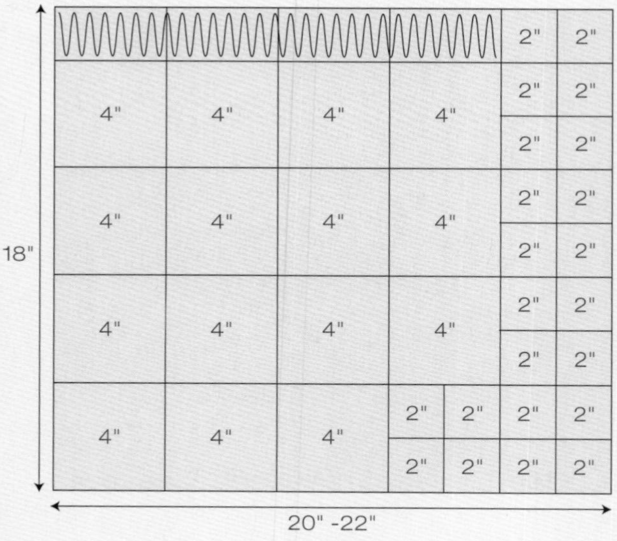

Fat quarter cutting diagram.

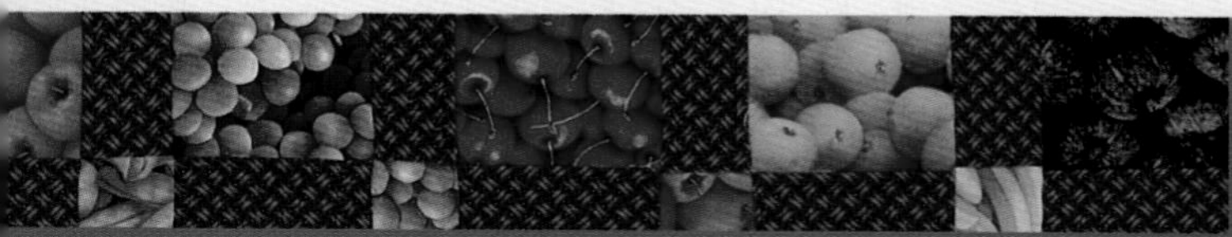

assemble the top

[1] Working on a design wall or on the floor, lay out the 4" squares in 16 rows of 12 blocks each, leaving space between the blocks for sashing and cornerstones. Lay the fabrics out in a random fashion. You will want to avoid having two like fabrics touching.

[2] Add the cornerstones to the design, again placing fabrics in a random fashion and avoiding creating areas with groups of the same fabrics in close proximity.

[3] Once the blocks are laid out in a pleasing manner, lay the sashing fabric between the blocks.

[4] Join the sashing and blocks together into rows.

[5] Press the seams in each row in opposite directions. This will allow the seams in each row to nest with the seams in the row below it. *Alternate pressing suggestion*: Press all seams toward the sashing fabric, if desired.

[6] Join the rows together. Press.

[7] Stay stitch the edges of the quilt top.

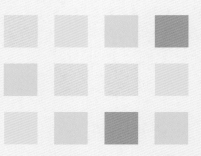

Lay out the blocks in a pleasing manner.

Assemble the quilt.

· TIP · TIP · TIP · TIP · TIP · TIP ·

Staystitching stabilizes the edges of the quilt top. A pieced quilt top that doesn't have borders often has many seams along the edges. As you handle the quilt top while basting and quilting it, the stitching at the end of these seams has a tendency to pull apart. To stay stitch, stitch around the outside of your quilt a scant ¼" from the edge. This line of stitching will be covered when you apply your binding.

prepare the backing

[1] Cut the backing fabric into two equal pieces.

[2] Remove the selvedges and join the pieces together.

finish

[1] Prepare your quilt sandwich following the Layering and Basting instructions on page 12.

[2] Quilt. If you used novelty prints as your blocks and would like to accent them, you could leave the large blocks unquilted and quilt a serpentine or stipple in the sashings. In the black and red variation, horizontal and diagonal lines were quilted throughout.

bind

Bind following the Binding instructions on page 12.

label

If you chose a novelty fabric for your quilt, why not carry out the theme on your label? For the fruit and vegetable quilt, I made a label in the shape of a carrot. In the Asian-inspired quilt, gingko leaves were a recurring theme, so a label in the shape of a gingko leaf seemed appropriate.

Layout diagram.

twelfth
night

In this charming quilt, the fat quarters make up the background and the accent fabric is the "star." The entire quilt is made with squares and half-square triangles. The big stitch technique is a nice way to finish this quilt.

variations

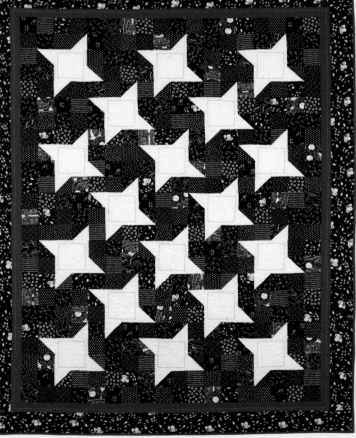

A touch of red gives life to the otherwise monochromatic tone of this quilt.
PIECED AND QUILTED BY THE AUTHOR, BIG STITCH BY BEVERLY WAKEMAN, 2005.

The addition of a big stitch outline sets off the stars in this quilt.
PIECED BY ETHEL KNAPP AND QUILTED BY THE AUTHOR, BIG STITCH BY BEVERLY WAKEMAN, 2005.

choosing fabric

The background in this design comes from the fabrics in the fat quarter bundle, and the stars are made from an accent fabric. The fabrics in the bundle of fat quarters you choose for this quilt need to be of the same value. A monochromatic color scheme would work nicely, but you don't need to be limited to one color. It is the value that is critical here.

The narrow inner border can be made from the same fabric as the stars, or choose something radically different, such as red for a black and white quilt or gold for a blue and white quilt. The outside border can tie everything together again if you pick a color that was used in the body of the quilt.

Some good combinations for this quilt would be a background made of 1930s reproductions with white stars, multiple blues for the background with yellow or gold stars, or white and cream background fabrics with red prints for the stars.

measurements

Quilt: 55" x 70"

Block: 2½" square

fabric requirements

12 fat quarters

1 yd. accent fabric for the stars

½ yd. inner border fabric

1 yd. outer border fabric

3½ yd. backing fabric

⅝ yd. binding fabric

54" x 74" batting

· TIP · TIP · TIP · TIP ·

Value is the intensity of color, not the color itself. You can purchase a value finder to help you determine the value of your fabrics. When you look at fabrics through this little red lens, it takes away the color and lets you see if some of the fabrics are lighter or darker than others.

cutting instructions

NOTE: Place the 20"-22" side of the fat quarters along the bottom of your cutting mat, selvedge at the right.

From each fat quarter, cut:

    5 (3") strips; crosscut into 25 (3") squares

    1 (3⅜") strip; crosscut into 5 (3⅜") squares

From the accent fabric, cut:

    6 (3") strips; crosscut into 78 (3") squares

    4 (3⅜") strips; crosscut in 44 (3⅜") squares

From the inner border, cut:

    6 (2") strips x width of fabric

From the outer border, cut:

    7 (4") strips x width of fabric

From the binding fabric, cut:

    7 (2¼") strips x width of fabric

Fat quarter cutting diagram.

piece the blocks

Make the half-square triangles for the star points:

[1] For the star points, draw a diagonal line from corner to corner on 36 of the 3⅜" background squares.

[2] Pair each of these with a 3⅜" square of star fabric, right sides together.

[3] Sew ¼" on either side of the marked line.

[4] Cut on the marked line. Press to the darker fabric.

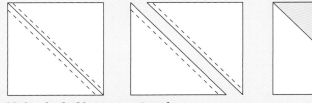

Make the half-square triangles.

assemble the top

[1] Working on a design wall or on the floor, lay out the background squares, the star points and the squares for the star centers. Refer to the layout diagram for the placement. Spread the background squares throughout the quilt in a random fashion. You will want to avoid having two like fabrics touching.

[2] Once you have the blocks laid out in a pleasing manner, join the blocks together into rows.

[3] Press the seams in each row in opposite directions. This will allow the seams in each row to nest with the seams in the row below it.

[4] Join the rows together. Press.

add the borders

[1] Join the strips for the inner border together by sewing diagonal seams. Press open. Join all of the strips together until you have one long strip.

[2] Measure the quilt lengthwise *through the middle*. This will prevent you from having wavy borders. Mathematically this number would be 60½", but everyone's seam allowances vary, so be sure to measure.

[3] Cut two strips the length of the quilt.

[4] Attach one to each side of the quilt. Press.

[5] Measure the quilt crosswise *through the middle*. This measurement should be approximately 48½", but check your measurement to be sure.

[6] Cut two strips this length.

[7] Attach one strip to the top and one to the bottom of the quilt. Press.

[8] Repeat Steps 1-7 with the outer border fabric.

prepare the backing

[1] Cut the backing fabric into two equal pieces.

[2] Remove the selvedges and join the pieces together.

---

finish

[1] Prepare your quilt sandwich following the Layering and Basting instructions on page 12.

[2] Quilt. You could do a combination of hand and machine quilting on this quilt. You could machine quilt in the background and outline quilt the stars by hand. You may want to try quilting the stars with the big stitch technique.

· TIP · TIP · TIP · TIP · TIP · TIP ·

Big stitch is a decorative quilting stitch done by hand. It is generally done with size 8 pearl cotton floss. As its name implies, the stitches are large. Historically called the "depression stitch" or "utility stitch," this manner of quilting is much faster than fine hand quilting. Besides being utilitarian, it can also be quite decorative.

To do this type of stitching, thread a size 5 needle with the pearl cotton floss. Make a stitch about ¼" long on the top of the quilt, and smaller on the bottom of the quilt. For the best result, try to keep the stitch size consistent.

---

bind

Bind following the Binding instructions on page 12.

---

label

You have enough squares left from piecing your top to make one more star block. This would be a perfect label for your quilt.

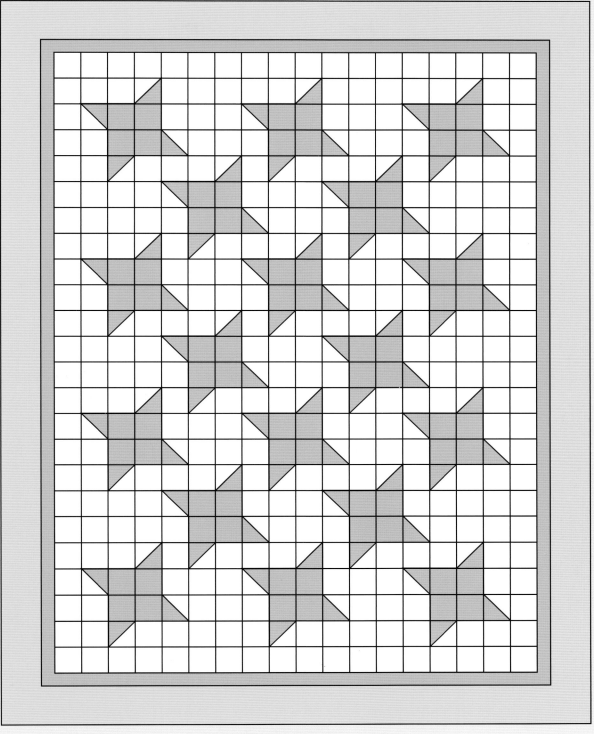

Layout diagram.

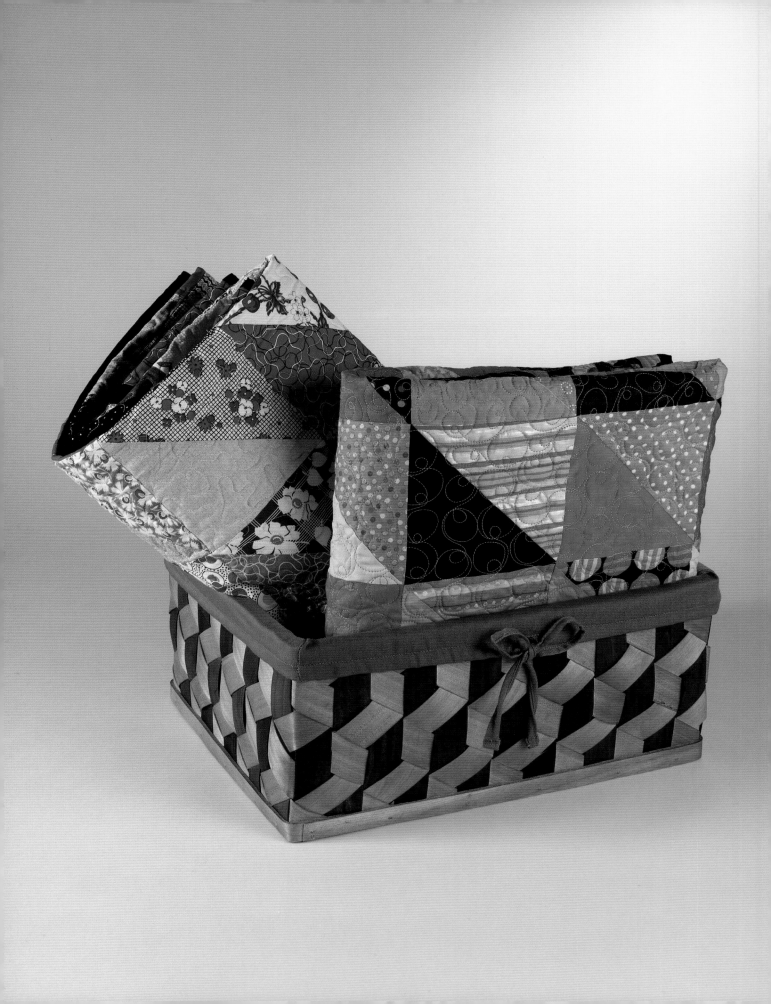

two
twelve
packs

This quilt requires two bundles — or 24 — fat quarters. It offers a great opportunity to combine a bundle of prints and a bundle of "solids." Using 24 fat quarters yields a quilt that is large enough for a twin bed with blocks left over to make a matching pillow sham.

When I first made this pattern, however, I had something else in mind; I was in need of two baby quilts. The half-square triangles were quick to piece and easy to divide for two quilts. If you know you have a baby quilt to make, why not choose this pattern? You'll have two baby quilts finished in no time — one to give away now and one ready when you get the announcement that the next baby is on the way.

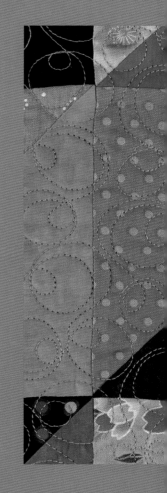

variations

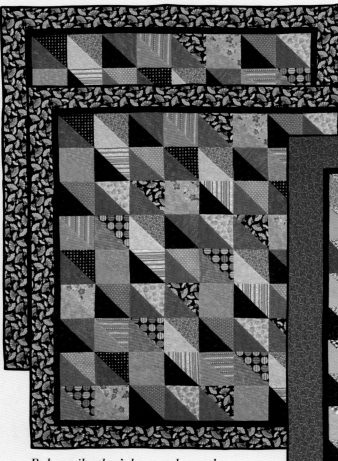

Bold floral fabrics reminiscent of the 1940s make a quilt that would look charming on a vintage bed.
PIECED BY MELINDA CROWLEY AND QUILTED BY THE AUTHOR, 2005.

Baby quilts don't have to be made from pastels. In fact, studies show that the first "colors" baby sees are black and white.
PIECED AND QUILTED BY THE AUTHOR, 2005.

choosing fabric

This quilt offers an opportunity to use two bundles of fat quarters. Make sure there is good contrast between the two bundles. One way to do this is to pick a bundle that has a lot going on in the fabrics, like multi-colored florals or busy novelty prints. For your second bundle, pick fabrics that are solid, or "read" as solid. It's a good idea to have your solids a different value than your prints. For example, if your prints are medium in value, choose solids that have a darker value. If you can't find two bundles of fat quarters that work together, pick a bundle of print fabrics and choose "solids" off the bolt to go with it.

These quilts have pieced backings. In order to make the back of the quilts from a single length of fabric, you will use strips left from cutting up your fat quarters. Just string them together, split the backing fabric, and insert them. You'll have an interesting surprise on the back of your quilt.

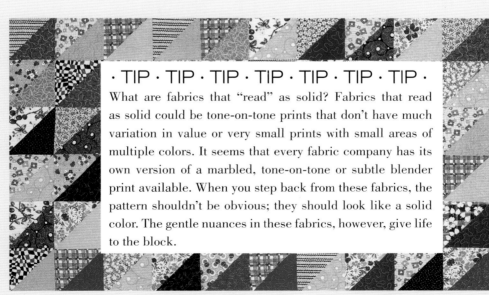

· TIP · TIP · TIP · TIP · TIP · TIP · TIP ·

What are fabrics that "read" as solid? Fabrics that read as solid could be tone-on-tone prints that don't have much variation in value or very small prints with small areas of multiple colors. It seems that every fabric company has its own version of a marbled, tone-on-tone or subtle blender print available. When you step back from these fabrics, the pattern shouldn't be obvious; they should look like a solid color. The gentle nuances in these fabrics, however, give life to the block.

measurements

Baby quilts: each 53" x 58½"

Twin quilt: 60½" x 88"

Block: 5½" square

fabric requirements

FABRIC	BABY QUILTS	TWIN QUILT
Fat quarters	24	24
Inner border fabric	½ yd.	⅔ yd.
Outer border fabric	1½ yd.	1¼ yd.
Backing fabric	3½ yd.	2⅝ yd.
Muslin or white fabric	⅓ yd.	
Binding fabric	⅞ yd.	⅝ yd.
Batting	2 (57" x 63") pieces	64" x 92"

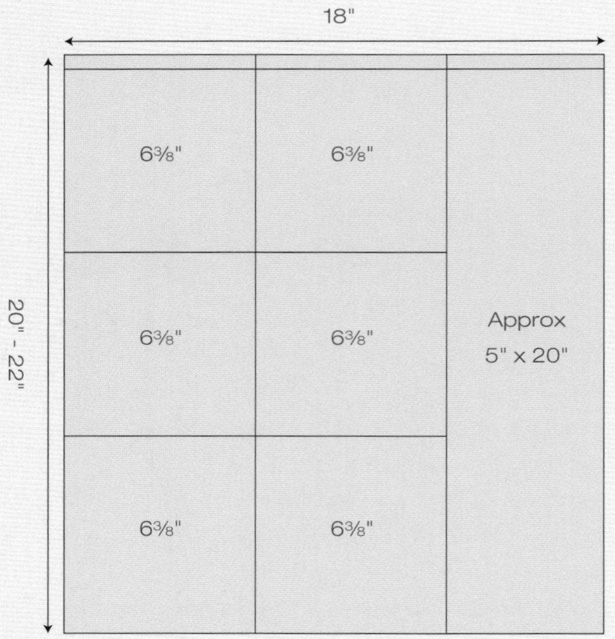
18"
20" - 22"
6⅜"
6⅜"
6⅜"
6⅜"
6⅜"
6⅜"
Approx
5" x 20"

Fat quarter cutting diagram.

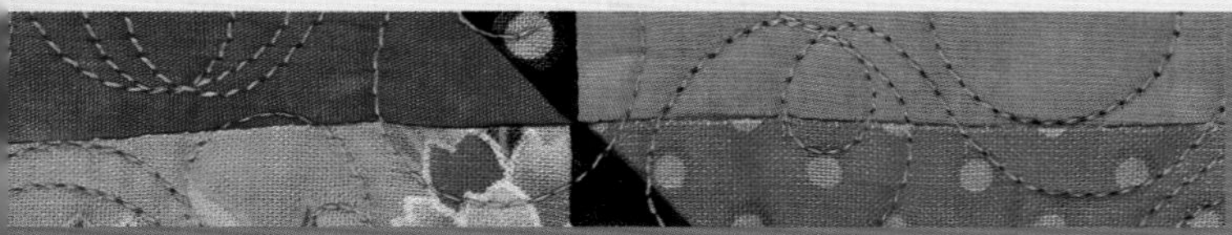

cutting instructions

NOTE: Place the 18" side of the fat quarter along the bottom edge of the cutting mat, selvedge at the top.

CUT	BABY QUILTS	TWIN QUILT
From each of the 24 fat quarters	2 (6⅜") strips; crosscut into 6 (6⅜") squares *Note:* You will have a strip left over that is approximately 5" x 20". Set this aside for use in the pieced backing.	2 (6⅜") strips; crosscut into 6 (6⅜") squares *Note:* You will have a strip left over that is approximately 5" x 20". Set this aside for use in the pieced backing.
From the inner border fabric	11 (1½") strips x width of fabric	7 (1½") strips x width of fabric
From the outer border fabric	11 (4") strips x width of fabric	8 (5") strips x width of fabric
From the muslin or white fabric	2 (5") strips; crosscut into 4 (5" x 20-21") pieces	
From the binding	12 (2¼") strips x width of fabric	9 (2¼") strips x width of fabric

piece the blocks

[1] On the back of half of the squares (choose either the print or the solids — whichever is easier to mark), draw a diagonal line. Randomly pair print and solid squares, right sides together.

[2] Stitch a scant ¼" on either side of the drawn line.

[3] Once all squares are sewn, cut apart on drawn line. This will yield 144 half-square triangles; each square should be 6". Press with seams to the solid fabric.

Make half-square triangles.

assemble the top

To assemble two baby quilts:

[1] Divide the half-square triangle blocks into two stacks of 72 blocks each.

[2] Working on a design wall or on the floor, lay out one stack of blocks in nine rows of eight blocks each. Arrange the blocks in a random fashion, keeping the solid side of the block to the top right (see layout diagram). This is a scrappy quilt, so anything goes, but you will want to avoid having two like fabrics touching whenever possible.

[3] Once you have the blocks laid out in a pleasing manner, join the blocks together into rows.

[4] Press the seams in each row in opposite directions. This will allow the seams in each row to nest with the seams in the row below it.

[5] Join the rows together. Press.

[6] Repeat Steps 1-5 for the second baby quilt.

To assemble the twin quilt:

[1] Working on a design wall or on the floor, lay out 14 rows of nine blocks each. Arrange the blocks in a random fashion, keeping the solid side of the block to the top right (see layout diagram). This is a scrappy quilt, so anything goes, but you will want to avoid having two like fabrics touching whenever possible.

[2] Once you have the blocks laid out in a pleasing manner, join the blocks together into rows.

[3] Press the seams in each row in opposite directions. This will allow the seams in each row to nest with the seams in the row below it.

[4] Join the rows together. Press.

add the borders

[1] Join the strips for the inner border together by sewing diagonal seams. Press open. Join all of the strips together until you have one long strip.

[2] Measure the quilt lengthwise *through the middle*. This will prevent you from having wavy borders. Mathematically this number would be 50" for the baby quilts (77½" for the twin quilt), but everyone's seam allowances vary, so be sure to measure.

[3] Cut two strips the length of the quilt.

[4] Attach one strip to each side of the quilt. Press.

[5] Measure the quilt crosswise *through the middle*. This measurement should be approximately 46½" for the baby quilts (52" for the twin quilt), but check your measurement to be sure.

[6] Cut two strips this length.

[7] Attach one strip to the top and one to the bottom of the quilt. Press.

[8] Repeat Steps 1-7 with the outer border fabric.

prepare the backing

For either size quilt:

[1] Randomly select prints and solids from the leftover pieces cut from the fat quarters.

[2] Sew them together along the longest side.

For the baby quilts:
Make two strip sets, inserting two of the muslin strips randomly among the others. These will serve as a label for your quilt.

For the twin quilt:
Make one long strip set. If desired, add a muslin strip for a label.

· TIP · TIP · TIP · TIP · TIP · TIP · TIP · TIP · TIP · TIP · TIP · TIP · TIP ·

When sewing strips together, there may be a slight variation in their length. To get the best use of your fabric, keep the top edges of the strips even.

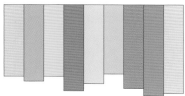

Piece the strips together.

For the baby quilts:

[1] Using a rotary cutter, even the edges of the strip-pieced units.

[2] Divide the backing fabric into two 63" pieces. Set one piece aside for the second quilt.

[3] Split the backing fabric lengthwise.

[4] Insert the stripped piece between the two sections of backing fabric. Stitch.

[5] Repeat with the second baby quilt back. Your quilt backs will be approximately 60" x 63."

For the twin quilt:

[1] Using a rotary cutter, even the edges of the strip-pieced unit.

[2] Split the backing fabric lengthwise.

[3] Insert the strip-pieced unit between the two sections of backing fabric.

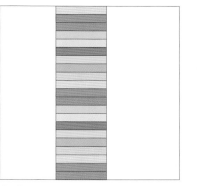

[3] *Pieced back.*

finish

[1] Prepare your quilt sandwich following the Layering and Basting instructions on page 12.

[2] Quilt. An overall quilting design would look good on this quilt. Often a quilting design with lots of curves creates a nice counterpoint to the straight lines of the pieced blocks. As an alternative, you could quilt only in the solid triangles, giving added dimension to the unquilted triangles.

bind

Bind following the Binding instructions on page 12.

label

Be sure to use a strip on the back of your quilt as a label. On the baby quilts, there will be two strips that you can use. On one of them, you may wish to write the information about you, the quiltmaker. On the other, you could write the baby's name, date of birth and weight.

Twin quilt layout diagram.

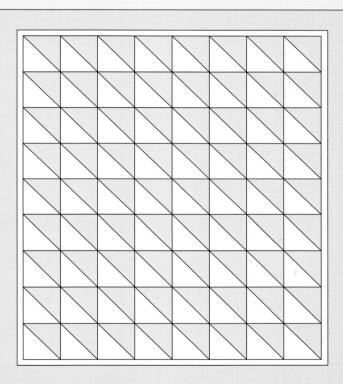

Baby quilt layout diagram.

Make 2.

bonus pillow shams

With very little effort, you can make two pillow shams that coordinate with the twin-sized quilt. A little additional fabric and the blocks left over after assembling the twin quilt are all you need. These lap-backed shams take so little time to make and the result is a wonderful ensemble.

measurements

Shams: each 22" x 26"

fabric requirements

(For two shams)

16 (5½") squares left over after assembling the twin quilt top

1¼ yd. main fabric

½ yd. accent fabric

cutting instructions

From the main fabric, cut:
2 (22½") strips; crosscut each strip into 2 (15½" x 22½") pieces and 1 (11½" x 22½") piece

From the accent fabric, cut:
8 (1½") strips; trim each to 1½" x 22½"

assemble the pillow sham

[1] From the leftover blocks, sew four strip sets of four blocks each.

[2] Referring to the layout diagram below, assemble the following pieces:

- One 15½" piece of the main fabric
- One 1½" strip of accent fabric
- One strip set of pieced blocks
- One 1½" strip of accent fabric
- One 11½" piece of the main fabric
- One 1½" strip of accent fabric
- One strip set of pieced blocks
- One 1½" strip of accent fabric
- One 15½" piece of the main fabric

[3] Press seams toward the accent strips.

[4] On each short end, press under a double ¼" hem.

[5] Topstitch each hem.

[6] Lay the sham right-side up. Bring each end toward the middle, folding where it meets the first accent strip; the center will overlap.

[7] Pin the long edges and stitch. Reinforce where the pieces overlap with extra stitching.

[8] Turn the sham right-side out.

[9] Repeat Steps 1-8 for the second sham.

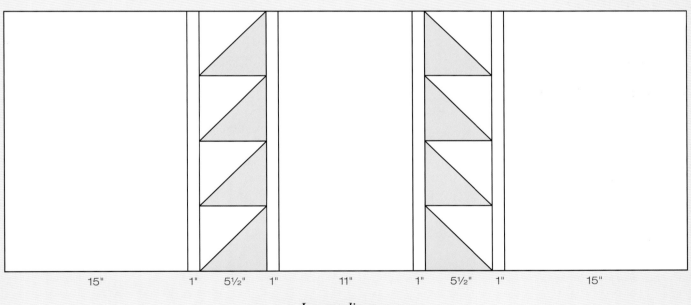

| 15" | | 1" | 5½" | 1" | 11" | 1" | 5½" | 1" | 15" |

Layout diagram.

midnight cowboy

Growing up, I was a "horse crazy" girl and haven't quite outgrown it! My girlfriend Diann and I would ride our horses on the beach every day we could. When we weren't riding, we were reading about horses. We even vowed we would get married on horseback. While I didn't go quite that far, I did have a Western-themed wedding! For this quilt, you have two options: you can choose a bundle of fat quarters that has four light fabrics and eight dark fabrics, or you can choose a bundle that is more monochromatic and add an accent fabric.

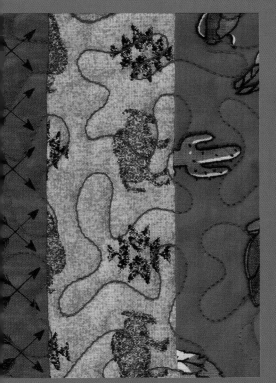

variations

This small quilt would surely please any little cowpoke.
PIECED AND QUILTED BY THE AUTHOR, 2005.

Blue and yellow fabrics create a summery feel in this quilt.
PIECED BY KAREN HARMON AND QUILTED BY THE AUTHOR, 2005.

Fun colors and novelty prints make this quilt a crowd-pleaser.
PIECED BY CORTNÉ STRICKER AND QUILTED BY THE AUTHOR, 2005.

choosing fabric

Contrast is the key to success when making this quilt. If you are making the smaller version, be sure you choose eight fat quarters that are medium to dark in value, and four that are light in value. If you'd rather make the larger quilt, choose a bundle of fat quarters that have the same value and add an accent fabric that stands out.

If you're using a bundle of cowboy prints, how about adding an accent fabric that shows different cattle brands or lariats? You don't need to be limited to cowboy prints for this quilt. As long as you establish good contrast, you could choose any fabrics. Why not try red, white and blue for a patriotic theme or blues and yellows for an elegant look?

measurements

Quilt: 57" x 66" for Option 1 (or 70½" x 75" for Option 2)

Block: 4½" square

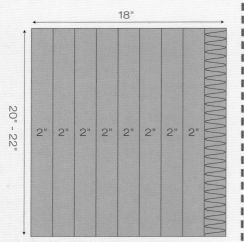

Fat quarter cutting diagram.

fabric requirements

FABRIC	OPTION 1: LIGHT AND DARK FABRICS	OPTION 2: MONOCHROMATIC FABRICS WITH ACCENT
Fat quarters	12	12
Accent fabric		1½ yd.
Inner border fabric	½ yd.	½ yd.
Outer border fabric	1 yd.	1¼ yd.
Backing fabric	3⅔ yd.	4¾ yd.
Binding fabric	½ yd.	⅔ yd.
Batting	61" x 70"	75" x 79"

cutting instructions

NOTE: Place the 18" side of the fat quarter along the bottom edge of your cutting mat, selvedge at the top.

CUT	OPTION 1: LIGHT AND DARK FABRICS	OPTION 2: MONOCHROMATIC FABRIC WITH ACCENT
From each of the 12 fat quarters	8 (2") strips; strips will need to be at least 20" long	8 (2") strips; strips will need to be at least 20" long
From the accent fabric		24 (2") strips x width of fabric; cut each strip in half to yield 48 (2" x 22") strips
From the inner border fabric	6 (2") strips x width of fabric	7 (2") strips x width of fabric
From the outer border fabric	6 (5") strips x width of fabric	8 (5") strips x width of fabric
From the binding fabric	7 (2¼") strips x width of fabric	8 (2¼") strips x width of fabric

piece the blocks

[1] Separate the strips into two piles, with the accent fabric in one pile and the other fabrics in another pile; you should have half as many accent strips as the other strips.

[2] Randomly join three strips into strip sets. The middle strip should always be the accent fabric.

[3] Repeat until you have 32 strip sets for Option 1 (48 strip sets for Option 2).

[4] Cut the strip sets into 5" segments. You will need four 5" segments from each strip set; this will yield 128 segments for Option 1 (192 segments for Option 2).

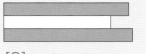

[2] *Piece strip sets.*

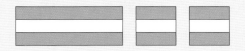

[4] *Cut segments.*

assemble the top

[1] Working on a design wall or on the floor, lay out the blocks in 12 rows of 10 blocks each for Option 1 (14 rows of 13 blocks each for Option 2). Alternate the blocks so the direction of the strips in each block is horizontal, vertical, horizontal, vertical, etc. Start odd rows with a horizontal block and even rows with a vertical block (see the layout diagram). Arrange the blocks in a random fashion. This is a scrappy quilt, so anything goes, but you will want to avoid having two like fabrics touching whenever possible.

[2] Once the blocks are laid out in a pleasing manner, join the blocks together into rows. You will have eight blocks left over for Option 1 (10 for Option 2).

[3] Press the seams in each row toward the vertical blocks. This will allow the seams in each row to nest with the seams in the row below it.

[4] Join the rows together. Press.

add the borders

[1] Join the strips for the inner border together by sewing diagonal seams. Press the seams open. Join all of the strips together until you have one long strip.

[2] Measure the quilt lengthwise *through the middle*. This will prevent you from having wavy borders. Mathematically this number would be 54½" for Option 1 (63½" for Option 2), but everyone's seam allowances vary, so be sure to measure.

[3] Cut two strips the length of the quilt.

[4] Attach one to each side of the quilt. Press.

[5] Measure the quilt crosswise *through the middle*. This measurement should be approximately 48½" for Option 1 (62" for Option 2), but check your measurement to be sure.

[6] Cut two strips this length.

[7] Add the strips to the top and bottom of the quilt. Press.

[8] Repeat Steps 1-7 with the outer border fabric.

prepare the backing

[1] Cut the backing fabric into two equal pieces.

[2] Remove the selvedges and join the pieces together.

finish

[1] Prepare your quilt sandwich following the Layering and Basting instructions on page 12.

[2] Quilt. Depending on your fabric choice, the light areas in the middle of the blocks could lend themselves to some fancy quilting. If you are machine quilting, a pantograph or overall design would work well. You could also quilt a continuous line through each strip, curving vertically and horizontally, following the strips in the blocks.

bind

Bind following the Binding instructions on page 12.

label

The light strip in the center of a rail fence block makes it the perfect signature block. If the fabric you chose for your center strips is light enough, record the pertinent information there. If it's too dark, substitute a piece of muslin. If there isn't enough room, use two!

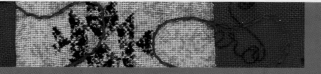

Layout diagram.

twelve step program

This is really a fun quilt to assemble. After sewing strips together to form a tube, you crosscut them, open them up and reassemble them to get the stair step effect. I once made this pattern for my secret pal at my quilt guild. I used some lovely William Morris fabrics, and instead of giving her a block each month, I gave her three strips.

variations

Hand-dyed batik fabrics give a rich look to this quilt.
PIECED BY JANET KING AND QUILTED BY THE AUTHOR, 2005.

The organic patterns created by 19th century designer William Morris are still popular today.
PIECED AND QUILTED BY THE AUTHOR, 2005.

choosing fabric

With the exception of borders, you won't be adding any additional fabrics to this quilt. In order for the stair step pattern to be effective, there needs to be some contrast to the fabrics when they are laid side by side. This contrast can be subtle, however, as in the William Morris quilt. For a quilt with sharper contrast, you could choose solid fabrics in an Amish palette. Another option would be to use six distinctively light and six distinctively dark fabrics, such as six red prints and six cream prints.

measurements

Quilt: 65" x 67"

fabric requirements

12 fat quarters

⅜ yd. inner border fabric

1¼ yd. outer border fabric

4 yd. backing fabric

½ yd. binding fabric

64" x 66" batting

additional materials

Masking tape or sticky dots

cutting instructions

NOTE: Place the 20"-22" side of your fat quarters along the bottom edge of your cutting mat, selvedge at the right.

From each of the 12 fat quarters, cut:

    4 (5") strips

From the inner border fabric, cut:

    6 (1½") strips x width of fabric

From the outer border fabric, cut:

    7 (5") strips x width of fabric

From the binding fabric, cut:

    8 (2¼") strips x width of fabric

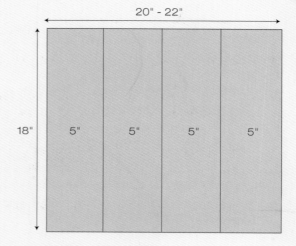

Fat quarter cutting diagram.

piece the strips

[1] Stack the fabric strips into 12 piles, having the same prints in each pile. You will have four strips in each pile.

[2] Lay the piles side by side, arranging them in a manner that is pleasing to you.

[3] Starting with the first pile, sew the long side of one strip to a strip from the next pile, right sides together. Because you are going to crosscut these sets, use about 15 stitches per inch.

[4] Continue until you have sewn 12 different strips together; this is a set.

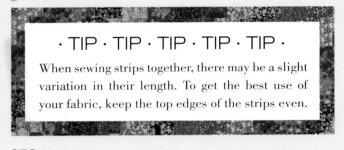

· TIP · TIP · TIP · TIP · TIP ·

When sewing strips together, there may be a slight variation in their length. To get the best use of your fabric, keep the top edges of the strips even.

[5] Press all seams of the set in one direction, being careful not to distort your fabric.

[6] Make a tube by sewing the first piece to the last piece. Press this seam in the same direction as the others.

[7] Repeat Steps 1-6 until the strips are gone, keeping your strips in the same order. You should now have four matching sets, with 12 fabrics in each set.

[8] Lay one set on your cutting surface. Smooth the tube with your hands, making sure the seams lay straight. Cut 2½" strips across the set. You now have loops of bricks.

[9] Repeat Step 8 with each set. Each set should yield seven loops for a total of 28.

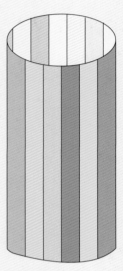

[6] *Sew the strips into a tube.*

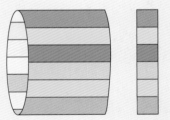

[8] *Cut the loops to yield loops of bricks.*

assemble the top

[1] Working on a long work surface like an uncluttered table or the floor, lay the loops side by side, with the same fabric at the top of each loop.

[2] Working from left to right, refold the loops. Leave the first loop just as it is. Fold the second loop under one-half block. Fold the third loop under one full block. Continue on in this manner — folding an additional half block each time — until you have refolded all the loops. A diagonal design will begin to appear as you work down the loops.

[3] Using masking tape or "sticky dots," number each loop 1-28, placing the number at the top.

[4] Cut each loop apart at the top fold in the following manner: cut the first loop at the seam line, just barely cutting more than the seam; cut the second loop in the center of the block, where you have folded it; cut the third loop on the seam line. Continue in this manner until you have cut each loop apart.

[5] Sew the pieces together in the order you have numbered them. Be careful to keep the short seams in one row in the middle of the block in the next row (see the layout diagram).

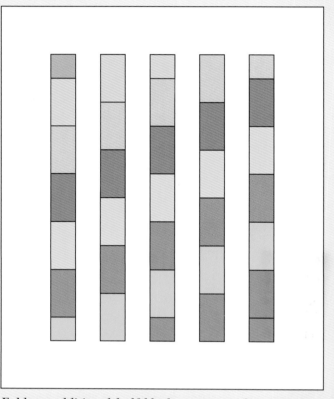

Fold an additional half block as you work across your loops.

add the borders

[1] Join the strips for the inner border together by sewing diagonal seams. Press open. Join all of the strips together until you have one long strip.

[2] Measure the quilt lengthwise *through the middle*. This will prevent you from having wavy borders. Mathematically, this number would be 56½", but everyone's seam allowances vary, so be sure to measure.

[3] Cut two strips the length of the quilt.

[4] Attach one to each side of the quilt. Press.

[5] Measure the quilt crosswise *through the middle*. This measurement should be approximately 56½", but check your measurement to be sure.

[6] Cut two strips this length.

[7] Add the strips to the top and bottom of the quilt. Press.

[8] Repeat Steps 1-7 with your outer border fabric.

prepare the backing

[1] Cut the backing fabric into two equal pieces.

[2] Remove the selvedges and join the pieces together.

finish

[1] Prepare your quilt sandwich following the Layering and Basting instructions on page 12.

[2] Quilt. A good option for this quilt would be to stitch in the ditch or stitch ¼" inside each block. An all-over design in a neutral thread would also be appropriate.

bind

Bind following the Binding instructions on page 12.

- -

label

Your quilt isn't finished until it has a label. Rubber stamps are an excellent way to embellish a quilt label. Permanent fabric ink is readily available. Use a stamp that reflects your personality or the personality of the quilt.

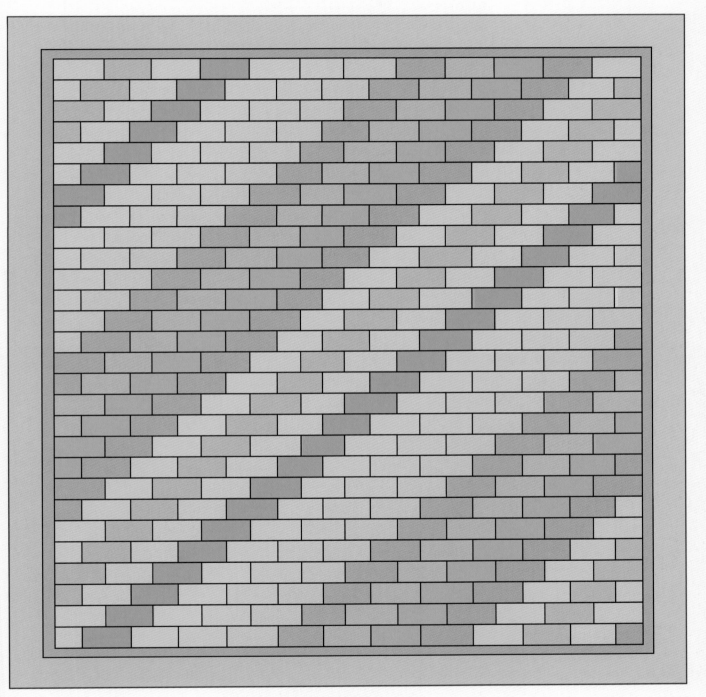

Layout diagram.

twelve drummers drumming

The blocks in this quilt create an interesting effect. Even though it is made only from squares with sew-and-flip corners, you get the illusion of curves! You could use just 12 fat quarters to make a wallhanging from this pattern or 12 fat quarters and an accent fabric for a larger throw. You have the option of making this quilt with or without borders.

The snowball is a very old pattern that was often used as a first or second quilt for young girls to stitch. Imagine the feeling of accomplishment when a quilt like this was finished!

variations

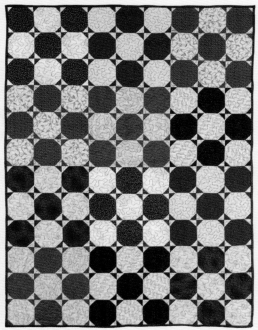

The warm tones used here result in a quilt with a country look.
PIECED AND QUILTED BY THE AUTHOR, 2005.

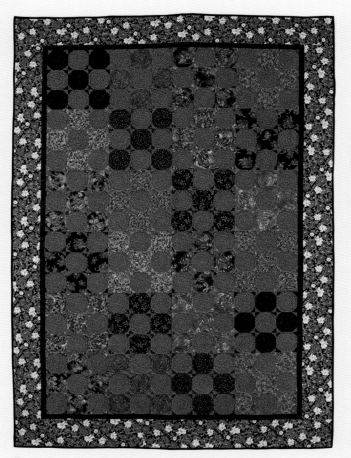

Bringing out a holiday quilt at Christmas can become a part of family tradition.
PIECED BY MONICA SOLORIO-SNOW AND QUILTED BY THE AUTHOR, 2005.

choosing fabric

If you choose to make the wallhanging, you will need a bundle of fat quarters that has an equal number of light and dark fabrics. If you are making the larger quilt, all the fat quarters will need to have a similar value; you will add a contrasting accent fabric.

Besides creating a Christmas theme with reds and greens, you could opt for a winter theme and choose a bundle of snowflake fabrics to make this quilt, playing on the traditional block name — snowball. You aren't limited to Christmas. This pattern could be made in tones of blue and beige or brights with black. Contrast is the key.

A border acts as a frame for a quilt. This quilt looks nice without a border, but the addition of a narrow inner border and a wider outer border will make your quilt larger and give it more visual weight.

measurements

Quilts without borders:
- Wallhanging: 36" x 48"
- Throw: 48" x 72"

Quilt with borders:
- Wallhanging: 46" x 58"
- Throw: 61" x 85"

Block: 12"

fabric requirements — quilts without borders

FABRIC	WALLHANGING	THROW
Fat quarters	12	12
Accent fabric		2¾ yd.
Binding	⅜ yd.	½ yd.
Backing	1⅝ yd.	3¼ yd.
Batting	40" x 52"	52" x 76"

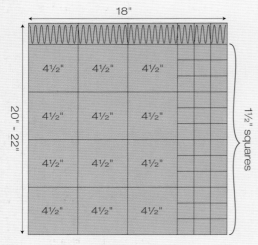

Fat quarter cutting diagram.

fabric requirements — quilts with borders

FABRIC	WALLHANGING	THROW
Fat quarters	12	12
Accent		2¾ yd.
Inner border	¼ yd.	⅝ yd.
Outer border	¾ yd.	1⅜ yd.
Binding	⅜ yd.	⅝ yd.
Backing	2⅛ yd.	5 yd.
Batting	50" x 62"	65" x 90"

cutting instructions — quilts without borders

NOTE: Place the 18" side of the fat quarter along the bottom edge of your cutting mat, selvedge at the top.

CUT	WALLHANGING	THROW
From each fat quarter	3 (4½") strips; crosscut into 12 (4½") squares. You will only use nine squares from each fat quarter. 3 (1½") strips; crosscut into 36 (1½") squares. *Note:* If you can't get three 1½" strips from your fat quarter, you can cut additional 1½" squares from the extra 4½" patches.	3 (4½") strips; crosscut into 12 (4½") squares. You will only use nine squares from each fat quarter. 3 (1½") strips; crosscut into 36 (1½") squares. *Note:* If you can't get three 1½" strips from your fat quarter, you can cut additional 1½" squares from the extra 4½" patches.
From the accent fabric		14 (4½") strips; crosscut into 108 (4½") squares
		16 (1½") strips; crosscut into 432 (1½") squares

cutting instructions — quilts with borders

NOTE: To add borders, follow the cutting instructions above *in addition to* the following.

CUT	WALLHANGING	THROW
From the inner border fabric	5 (1½") strips x width of fabric	8 (2") strips x width of fabric
From the outer border fabric	5 (4½") strips x width of fabric	8 (5½") strips x width of fabric
From the binding fabric	5 (2¼") strips x width of fabric	8 (2¼") strips x width of fabric

piece the blocks

NOTE: All instructions in ( ) are for the throw-size quilt.

[1] Make six piles of lights and six piles of darks, keeping like fabrics together for the wallhanging (or make 12 piles of fat quarter fabrics and place and equal amount of accent fabric with it for the throw).

[2] Pair each light pile with a dark pile. These two fabrics will be sewn to each other to make the blocks.

[3] Working with one pile of light/dark pairs for the wall-hanging (or one pile of fat quarters and accent fabric for the throw) sew a dark 1½" square to each corner of the light 4½" square. Carefully place each small square on a corner of the larger square, right sides together. Stitch diagonally from corner to corner on the small square. If you have difficulty sewing from corner to corner in a straight line, you can mark your small square with a pencil, or press it from corner to corner for a guide.

[4] Repeat with dark 4½" squares, sewing a light 1½" square to each corner.

[5] Open each small square to see if it lines up with the corner of the large square. If it does, trim away the excess corner, leaving a ¼" seam allowance. This can be done with scissors or a rotary cutter.

[6] Press the small triangles open. Press to the dark on both large and small squares. Take care not to stretch the bias on your blocks. You will have nine dark snowball blocks and nine light snowball blocks.

[7] From the snowball blocks, make two nine-patch blocks. One will have dark blocks on the outer corners and one will have light blocks on the outer corners.

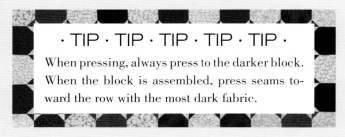

· TIP · TIP · TIP · TIP · TIP ·

When pressing, always press to the darker block. When the block is assembled, press seams toward the row with the most dark fabric.

[8] Repeat Steps 1-7, making two nine-patch blocks from each light/dark pile (all of the fat quarter piles).

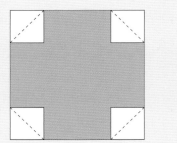 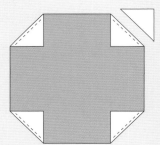

[3]-[4] *Add the corners.*   [5] *Trim the corners.*

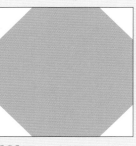

[6] *The snowball.*

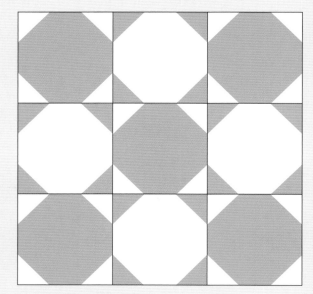

[7] *Piece the block.*

assemble the top

[1] Working on a design wall or on the floor, lay out the nine-patch blocks in four rows of three blocks each for the wallhanging (six rows of four blocks each for the throw). Lay them out in a random fashion, alternating blocks with light and dark corners. Remember, this is a scrappy quilt, so anything goes, but you will want to avoid having two like blocks together.

[2] Once you have the blocks laid out in a pleasing manner, join the blocks together into rows.

[3] Press the seams in each row in opposite directions. This will allow the seams in each row to nest with the seams in the row below it.

[4] Join the rows together. Press.

add the optional borders

[1] Join the strips for the inner border together by sewing diagonal seams. Press open. Join all of the strips together until you have one long strip.

[2] Measure the quilt lengthwise *through the middle*. This will prevent you from having wavy borders. Mathematically this number would be 48½" for the wallhanging (72½" for the throw), but everyone's seam allowances vary, so be sure to measure.

[3] Cut two strips the length of the quilt.

[4] Attach one to each side of the quilt. Press.

[5] Measure the quilt crosswise *through the middle*. This measurement should be approximately 38½" for the wallhanging (50½" for the throw), but check your measurement to be sure.

[6] Cut two strips this length.

[7] Add the strips to the top and bottom of the quilt. Press.

[8] Repeat Steps 1-7 with the outer border fabric.

prepare the backing — quilts without borders

Wallhanging

[1] One length of fabric will suffice for the back without any piecing.

Throw

[1] Cut the backing fabric into two equal pieces.

[2] Remove the selvedge and stitch the two pieces together along the longest sides.

preparing the backing — quilts with borders

Wallhanging

[1] From the backing fabric, cut a piece 26" long. Cut this piece along the fold, yielding two sections, each approximately 22" x 26". Remove the selvedges. Sew two short ends together to yield a piece approximately 22" x 51".

[2] The remaining piece of backing fabric should be approximately 50" long. Split this piece along the fold, yielding two sections, each approximately 22" x 50" long. Remove the selvedges. Insert the pieced section from Step 1.

Throw

[1] Cut the backing fabric into two equal pieces.

[2] Remove the selvedges and stitch the two pieces together along the longest sides.

finish

[1] Prepare your quilt sandwich following the Layering and Basting instructions on page 12.

[2] Quilt. The large areas in the snowballs make a nice area for some special quilting. You could quilt a star in each one, or a spiral. Let the fabric in your quilt help you make the decision about the quilting.

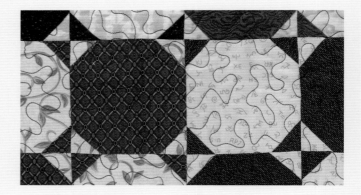

bind

Bind following the Binding instructions on page 12.

label

A snowball block makes a perfect quilt label. It would also be the perfect place to transfer a photograph. The corners of the snowball will act as a frame for your photo. Photo transfer paper is available at many quilt shops. Once the photo has been copied to the photo paper, a hot iron is all it takes to transfer it to fabric.

Throw layout diagram.

Wallhanging layout diagram.

cheaper by the dozen

This quilt is peppered with stars! And while it may look complicated, the blocks are simply 4" squares. The trick to making the stars is the simple sew-and-flip construction of the sashing. Once the star points have been sewn to the rectangles and the cornerstones are added, the quilt can be constructed in rows. This type of construction is perfect for chain piecing.

variations

This quilt conjures up visions of a starry night.
PIECED BY MONICA SOLORIO-SNOW AND QUILTED BY THE AUTHOR, 2005.

Many of the Halloween prints used here glow in the dark for added fun.
PIECED BY JOAN STOLTZ AND QUILTED BY THE AUTHOR, 2005.

choosing fabric

The stars in this quilt need to stand out from the rest of the fabrics. This can be achieved by making them a different value or a different color than the fabrics in your fat quarter bundle.

Fabrics with a celestial theme seem to be available year after year. A bundle of these with a warm gold for the stars is stunning. However, you don't need to limit yourself to the traditional color of stars. How about making this quilt from a bundle of pastel prints with yellow stars or a patriotic theme of red and blue with white stars?

A dark fabric for the narrow inner border creates nice separation between the body of the quilt and the outer border and makes a nice binding to frame the quilt. You may want to repeat one of the fabrics from the main body of the quilt in the outer border.

measurements

Quilt: 62" x 68"

Block: 4"

fabric requirements

12 fat quarters

1¾ yd. star fabric

1 yd. inner border and binding

1 yd. outer border fabric

3⅔ yd. backing

66" x 72" batting

· TIP · TIP · TIP · TIP · TIP ·

From the fat quarters, you will need a total of:

QUANTITY	SIZE	NAME
4	1½" squares	A
72	4½" squares	C
38	1½" x 2½" rectangles	D
34	1½" x 4½" rectangles	E
161	2½" x 4½" rectangles	F

From the star fabric, you will need:

QUANTITY	SIZE	NAME
90	2½" squares	B
720	1½" squares	G

cutting instructions

NOTE: Lay the 20"-22" side of your fat quarter along the bottom edge of your cutting mat, selvedge at the right.

Fat quarter cutting diagram.

From each of the 12 fat quarters, cut:

4 (4½") strips; crosscut 2 of the 4½" strips into 14 (4½" x 2½") rectangles (F); crosscut the 2 remaining strips into:

- 6 (4½") squares (C)
- 3 (4½" x 1½") rectangles (E)
- 1 (1½") square (A)

1 (1½") strip; crosscut into 4 (1½" x 2½") rectangles (D)

From the star fabric, cut:

6 (2½") strips x width of fabric; crosscut into 90 (2½") squares (B)

28 (1½") strips x width of fabric; crosscut into 720 (1½") squares

From the inner border and binding fabric, cut:

6 (1½") strips x width of fabric for the inner border

8 (2¼") strips for the binding

From the outer border fabric, cut:

8 (4½") strips x width of fabric

piece the blocks

NOTE: Use the sew-and-flip technique; the star points need to be added to the sashing (F) and border (E) pieces (see the Sew-and-Flip instructions below).

[1] Add a star point to each corner of sashing pieces (F), using the sew-and-flip technique. You may chain piece this step, doing the first corner of all sashing pieces. Before moving on to the next corner, however, be sure to trim and press the corners already sewn. You will need 161 sashing pieces with star points.

[2] Add a star point to two corners of border pieces (E), using the sew-and-flip technique. You will need 34 border pieces with star points.

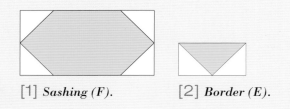

[1] Sashing (F).   *[2] Border (E).*

· TIP · TIP · TIP · TIP · TIP · TIP · TIP · TIP · TIP · TIP · TIP · TIP ·

Sew-and-Flip Corners

Sew-and-flip corners are an easy way to add a triangle to the corner of another piece of fabric without worrying about the stretch of a bias edge. It works great for making flying geese patches, or, in this case, the star points in the sashing.

You will need to make a mark or guide on the small squares of fabric used for the corners. You may do this by using a pencil and ruler and drawing the diagonal line on each square, or you may press each square in half diagonally and let the crease be your guide. You may also place a small piece of masking tape on the bed of your sewing machine, straight out from your needle, and let it be your guide.

The small square of fabric is then placed on the corner of the larger patch, right sides together, and a diagonal line is sewn across the small patch. The corner is trimmed away, leaving a ¼" seam allowance (this can be done with scissors or your rotary cutter). The triangle that remains is pressed over to replace the fabric that was cut away.

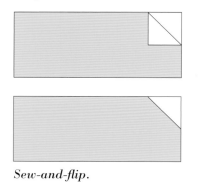

Sew-and-flip.

assemble the top

[1] Referring to the layout diagram, lay out the squares, sashes, posts and borders. Be sure that the different fabrics from your fat quarters are evenly distributed throughout your quilt.

[2] Once you have decided upon a layout, join the blocks together into rows.

[3] Press seams away from the star points in each row. This will allow the seams in each row to nest with the seams in the row below it.

[4] Join the rows together. Press.

add the borders

[1] Join the strips for the inner border together by sewing diagonal seams. Press open. Join all of the strips together until you have one long strip.

[2] Measure the quilt lengthwise *through the middle*. This will prevent you from having wavy borders. Mathematically this number would be 58½", but everyone's seam allowances vary, so be sure to measure.

[3] Cut two strips the length of the quilt.

[4] Attach one to each side of the quilt. Press.

[5] Measure the quilt crosswise *through the middle*. This measurement should be approximately 54½", but check your measurement to be sure.

[6] Cut two strips this length.

[7] Add them to the top and bottom of the quilt. Press.

[8] Repeat Steps 1-7 with the outer border fabric.

prepare the backing

[1] Cut your backing fabric into two equal pieces.

[2] Remove selvedges. Sew the long sides of the backing pieces together.

finish

[1] Prepare your quilt sandwich following the Layering and Basting instructions on page 12.

[2] Quilt. It is becoming more and more popular to use a combination of hand quilting and machine quilting when finishing projects. This would be a perfect candidate for combining the two. All of the background areas of the quilt could be stippled by machine. The stars could then be outline quilted by hand, ¼" from the seams, or the center of the stars could be quilted with a five-pointed star.

bind

Bind following the Binding instructions on page 12.

label

To add interest to your quilt label, you can use colored pens to recreate a motif from the fabrics used in your quilt. Pick a design in one of the fabrics you used and make a colored photocopy of it. Tape the photocopy to a desk or table, then tape your label fabric over the top. Using permanent markers trace the motif onto your label.

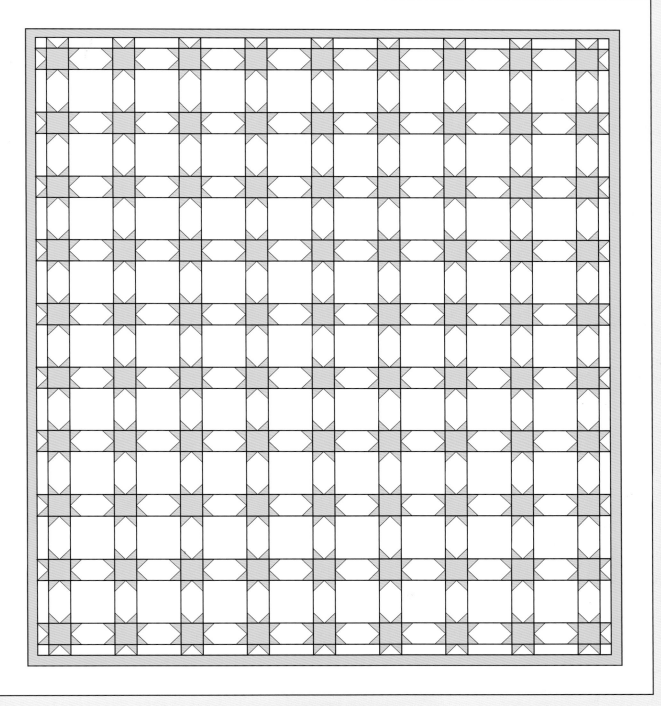

Layout diagram.

until the twelfth of never

Here's a quilt you can make using six light fat quarters and six dark fat quarters. Or, make it larger by using a bundle of 12 prints and adding 12 solid fabrics. The construction of this quilt requires only straight seams — no triangle or diamond points to match. It looks much more complicated than it really is, but by reversing the prints and solids in every other block, an interesting pattern appears, and no additional sashings or borders are needed. Thanks to Beverly Wakeman for sharing her design for this quilt.

variations

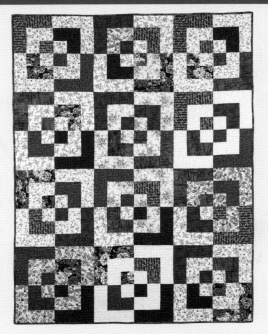

Pretty blue and white prints, reminiscent of fine china, create a fresh-looking quilt.
PIECED AND QUILTED BY THE AUTHOR, 2005.

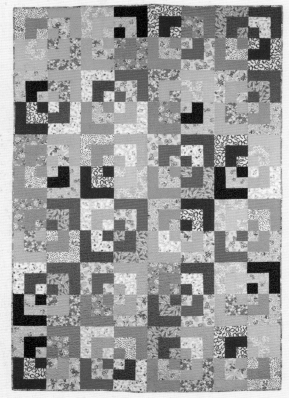

The large scale of these reproduction feed sack fabrics works well when combined with a variety of solids.
PIECED BY CONNIE NASON AND QUILTED BY THE AUTHOR, 2005.

The combination of floral fabrics in this quilt creates the look of a field of flowers.
PIECED BY KAREN HARMON AND QUILTED BY THE AUTHOR, 2005.

choosing fabric

This quilt requires no additional fabrics be added to the fat quarters, but you still have choices to make. The fabrics you choose will dramatically affect the outcome. To create crisp definition in the blocks of this quilt, choose fabrics with good contrast. Blacks paired with reds, or blues paired with oranges, would make striking quilts. If, however, you desire a quilt with a softer, muted look, choosing fabrics of similar value will give you the desired result.

measurements

Quilt: 45" x 60" for Option 1; 60" x 90" for Option 2
Block: 7½"

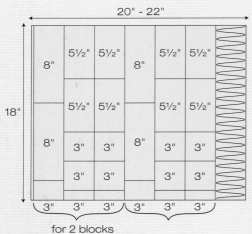

Fat quarter cutting diagram.

fabric requirements

FABRIC	OPTION 1: LIGHTS AND DARKS	OPTION 2: PRINTS AND SOLIDS
Fat quarters	12	24
Binding fabric	½ yd.	⅝ yd.
Backing fabric	2¾ yd.	5½ yd.
Batting	49" x 64"	64" x 94"

cutting instructions

NOTE: Lay out the fat quarters with the 20"-22" side along the bottom of your cutting mat, selvedge to the right.

CUT	OPTION 1: LIGHTS AND DARKS	OPTION 2: PRINTS AND SOLIDS
From each fat quarter	6 (3") strips; referring to the fat quarter cutting diagram, subcut into: 4 (3" x 8") rectangles 8 (3" x 5½") rectangles 8 (3") squares	6 (3") strips; referring to the fat quarter cutting diagram, subcut into: 4 (3" x 8") rectangles 8 (3" x 5½") rectangles 8 (3") squares
From the binding fabric	6 (2¼") strips	8 (2¼") strips

piece the blocks

[1] Sort your fabric pieces into 48 piles for Option 1 (96 piles for Option 2) — one for each block.

For each block you will need:

- one print and one solid 3" square
- one print and one solid 5½" rectangle
- one print **or** one solid 8" rectangle
- **NOTE:** The prints and solids in each block should be the same.

[2] Sew together a solid and print 3" square, right sides together. Press toward the solid.

[3] Place the print center square on the left. Add a solid 5½" rectangle on top. Sew and flip. Press toward the solid.

[4] Place the print center square on the lower left. Add a print 5½" rectangle on the right. Sew and flip. Press toward the solid.

[5] Place the print center square on the lower left. Add a print 8" rectangle on top. Sew and flip. Press to the mostly solid side. The blocks should be 8" square.

[6] Reverse the position of the solid and print fabrics and follow the same procedure (Steps 1-5) for piecing the dark blocks. Always press to the piece with the most solid. Piece 24 light and 24 dark blocks for Option 1 (48 light and 48 dark blocks for Option 2).

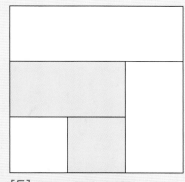

[5] *Piece the light block.*

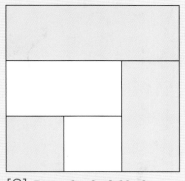

[6] *Piece the dark block.*

assemble the top

[1] Working on a design wall or on the floor, lay out the blocks in eight rows of six blocks each for Option 1 (12 rows of eight blocks each for Option 2). Lay them out in a random fashion. Odd rows alternate light and dark blocks with the center squares together on the bottom. Even rows alternate dark and light blocks with the center squares together on the top (see the layout diagram). Remember, this is a scrappy quilt, so anything goes, but you will want to avoid having two like blocks together.

[2] Once you have the blocks laid out in a pleasing manner, join the blocks together into rows.

[3] Press the seams toward the block with the most dark fabrics.

[4] Join the rows together. Press.

prepare the backing

[1] For either size quilt, cut your backing fabric into two equal pieces.

[2] Remove the selvedges and join the pieces together.

---

finish

[1] Prepare your quilt sandwich following the Layering and Basting instructions on page 12.

[2] Quilt. The geometric lines of this quilt would be enhanced by cross-hatching or quilting ¼" from all seams. Alternately, a nice counterpoint to the straight lines in the quilt would be a quilting pattern with many curving lines.

---

bind

Bind following the Binding instructions on page 12.

---

label

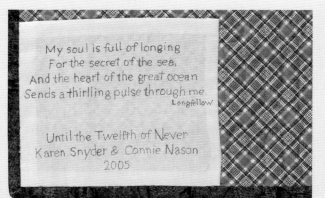

A label can include more than just the who, what, where and when of your quilt. If you have a favorite poem or quote that seems appropriate for the quilt or meaningful to the recipient, take a few extra minutes to add it to the label.

Layout diagram.

vitamin B-12

There seem to be as many basket patterns as there are star variations. Basket quilts have been perennial favorites among quiltmakers. This Cake Stand pattern seemed the perfect way to show off a bundle of polka-dot fat quarters. With the extra fabric from the fat quarters, you can create interesting sashing for this quilt. Monica Solorio-Snow gets the credit for coming up with this clever setting idea.

variations

Polka-dot fabrics against a crisp, white background result in a fresh look.
PIECED BY CONNIE NASON AND QUILTED BY THE AUTHOR, 2005.

An entirely different look is achieved when using solids from an Amish palette paired with black.
PIECED BY BEVERLY WAKEMAN AND QUILTED BY THE AUTHOR, 2005.

choosing fabric

The polka dot fabrics on a crisp, white background give this quilt a fresh, summer look. It would be just as successful made with blue fabrics on a white background, muted florals on a beige background or rich batiks on a black background. Find a bundle of fat quarters that speaks to you, then look for just the right background to show them off.

measurements

Quilt: 56" x 80"
Block: 10" square

fabric requirements

12 fat quarters

3⅛ yd. background and border fabric

3½ yd. backing fabric

⅝ yd. binding fabric

62" x 86" batting

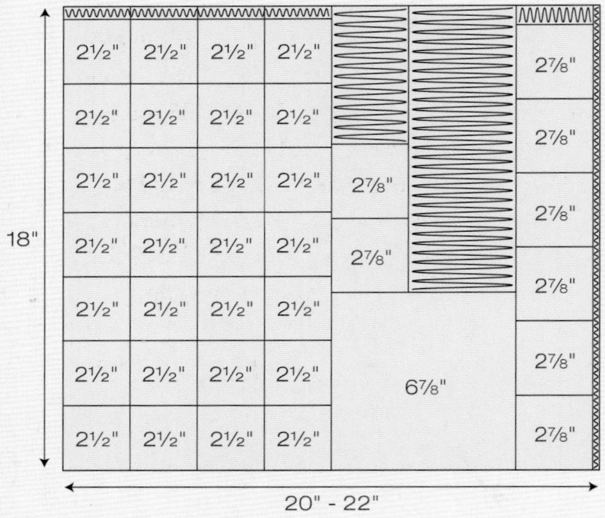

Fat quarter cutting diagram.

(diagram with dimensions: 18" height, 20" - 22" width; grid of 2½" squares, 2⅞" sections, and 6⅞" section)

cutting instructions

NOTE: Lay the fat quarters with the 20"–22" side along the bottom edge of your cutting mat, selvedge at the right.

From each fat quarter, cut:

    4 (2½") strips; crosscut into 28 (2½") squares for the sashing

    1 (6⅞") strip; crosscut into 1 (6⅞") square and 2 (2⅞") squares

    1 (2⅞") strip; crosscut into 6 (2⅞") squares

From the background fabric, cut:

    4 (2½") strips x width of fabric; crosscut into 59 (2½") squares

    Note: 24 of these squares will be used for piece (A) and 35 will be used as cornerstones in the sashing.

    6 (2⅞") strips x width of fabric; crosscut into 72 (2⅞") squares (B)

    8 (2½") strips x width of fabric; crosscut into 48 (2½" x 6½") rectangles (C)

    2 (4⅞") strips x width of fabric; crosscut into 12 (4⅞") squares; cut once diagonally to yield 24 triangles (D)

    3 (6⅞") strips x width of fabric; crosscut into 12 (6⅞") squares (E)

    7 (3½") strips x width of fabric for the border

From the binding fabric, cut:

    8 (2¼") strips

piece the blocks

· TIP · TIP · TIP · TIP · TIP · TIP · TIP · TIP · TIP · TIP ·

Each fat quarter will yield two blocks. The following instructions are for constructing two blocks from the same fabric at one time.

[1] On one 6⅞" square of background fabric, draw a diagonal line from corner to corner. Pair the square with a 6⅞" square of print fabric, right sides together.

[2] Stitch ¼" on each side of the drawn line. Cut apart on the pencil line. Trim the "dog ears." Press toward the print fabric. This yields two half-square triangles for the basket centers.

[3] On six 2⅞" squares of background fabric, draw a diagonal line from corner to corner. Pair each background square with a 2⅞" square from one fat quarter, right sides together.

[4] Stitch ¼" on each side of the drawn line. Cut apart on the pencil line. This yields 12 half-square triangles for the basket handles.

[5] Make four strips with three half-square triangles in each strip. Sew a 2½" square of background fabric to two of the strips as shown in the diagram below.

· TIP · TIP · TIP · TIP · TIP ·

"Dog ears" are the little points of fabric that extend beyond the seams when making half-square triangles. Trimming them makes a neater block and allows for easier matching of seams. A quick and easy way to trim dog ears is to place the pieced half-square triangle on a cutting mat before pressing it open. With the dog ears to the right and top, position a square ruler to the right top edge; cut off ears. The square is trimmed and the waste stays on the mat for easy cleanup.

[2] *Make half-square triangles.*

[5] *Make the handle sets.*

[6] Add the triangle strips to the basket centers as shown in the diagram at right.

[7] Sew a 2⅞" triangle to one end of four 2½" x 6½" background rectangles. *Note*: Use caution when adding the triangles. You will need to make pairs that are mirror images (refer to the basket base diagram for placement).

[8] Sew the rectangle units to the sides of the basket, checking to be sure the triangles form a base for the basket.

[9] Sew a 4⅞" background triangle to the base of each basket. To center the base triangle, fold the patch in half and finger press the long edge to mark the center. Match to the point of the large half-square triangle.

[10] Repeat with the fabrics from the other fat quarters. You will have 24 basket blocks.

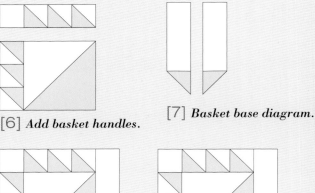

[6] *Add basket handles.*

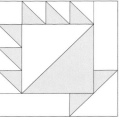

[7] *Basket base diagram.*

[8] *Add the basket base.*   [9] *Completed basket block.*

prepare the sashing

NOTE: The setting requires 58 sashing strips. These are made from the 2½" squares from the fat quarter fabrics.

[1] Randomly pick up two 2½" squares and sew them together to make pairs. Make 98 pairs.

[2] Divide the pairs into two equal piles. Sew them together to make strips, four patches across.

[3] Add an additional 2½" square to each strip. Make 58 sets.

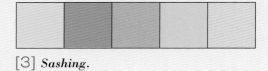

[3] *Sashing.*

assemble the top

[1] Working on a design wall or on the floor, lay out the basket blocks and the sashing strips. Insert a 2½" square of background fabric at each of the intersections. Be careful to turn all of your basket blocks in the same direction (see the layout diagram). You will want to avoid having two blocks made from the same fabric side by side.

[2] Once you have the blocks laid out in a pleasing manner, join the blocks and sashing together into rows.

[3] Press the seams toward the sashing. This will allow the seams in each row to nest with the seams in the row below it.

[4] Join the rows together. Press.

add the borders

[1] Join the strips for the inner border together by sewing diagonal seams. Press open. Join all of the strips together until you have one long strip.

[2] Measure the quilt lengthwise *through the middle*. This will prevent you from having wavy borders. Mathematically this number would be 74½", but everyone's seam allowances vary, so be sure to measure.

[3] Cut two strips the length of the quilt.

[4] Attach one to each side of the quilt. Press.

[5] Measure the quilt crosswise *through the middle*. This measurement should be approximately 56½", but check your measurement to be sure.

[6] Cut two strips this length.

[7] Add the strips to the top and bottom of the quilt. Press.

[8] Repeat Steps 1-7 with the outer border fabric.

prepare the backing

NOTE: You will cut your backing fabric into two unequal pieces.

[1] Cut one piece of backing fabric 42" long. Cut this piece along the fold, yielding two sections, each approximately 22" x 42". Remove the selvedges. Sew the two short ends together to yield a piece approximately 22" x 83½".

[2] The remaining piece of backing fabric should be approximately 84" long. Split this piece along the fold, yielding two sections, each approximately 22" x 84" long.

[3] Remove the selvedges. Insert the pieced section from Step 1.

[3] *Piece the backing.*

finish

[1] Prepare your quilt sandwich following the Layering and Basting instructions on page 12.

[2] Quilt. If you are machine quilting, this quilt would be a good candidate for stitching in the ditch. It would also work well to stipple the background fabric and leave the baskets unquilted. If you are hand quilting, the open area of the basket would make a perfect place to quilt some fruit or flowers and the remaining pieces could be outline quilted.

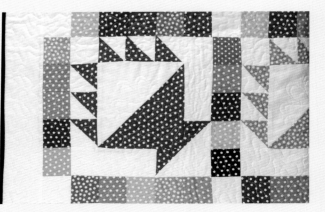

bind

Bind following the Binding instructions on page 12.

label

To give your quilt label more permanency, you can stitch it to the back of the quilt before binding. After quilting stitch the label to a corner of the back of the quilt. Apply the binding strips in the regular manner. When you turn the binding to the back of the quilt and stitch by hand, you will catch two edges of the label with the binding.

Layout diagram.

resources

Anna Lena's Quilt Shop
PO Box 1399
111 Bolstad Avenue
Long Beach, WA 98631
(360) 642-8585
www.annalena.com

Annie's Attic
1 Annie Lane
Big Sandy, TX 75755
(800) 582-6643
www.anniesattic.com

Keepsake Quilting
Route 25
P.O. Box 1618
Center Harbor, NH 03226-1618
(800) 438-5464
www.keepsakequilting.com

KP Books
(888) 457-2873
www.krause.com

about the author

Karen Snyder likes to say she was a child of the Fifties, when cakes were made from boxed mixes, Jell-O was considered a salad, and clothes and bedding were purchased ready-made. She always enjoyed being creative, however, and knew that someday she would be a quilter. In 1995, just after her forty-second birthday, she received a free quilt pattern in the mail, and decided if she was going to become a quilter, she'd better get started. Within three years, she had finished that quilt (a king-sized Grandmother's Flower Garden), made several more, and opened a quilt shop.

Besides being the owner of Anna Lena's Quilt Shop, Karen teaches quilting classes, writes patterns under the name History Stitchery, and designs fabric for Andover Fabrics. She and her husband, Bob Hamilton, live in beautiful Long Beach, Wash., the town she grew up in.